The Coming Night Is Full of Stars

Poetry and Prose
By Robert Pike

Photographs by
Carrie Pike

**Grosvenor House
Publishing Limited**

This book is published by
Grosvenor House Publishing Ltd
Link House
140 The Broadway, Tolworth, Surrey, KT6 7HT.
www.grosvenorhousepublishing.co.uk

A CIP record for this book
is available from the British Library

ISBN 978-1-83975-682-5

TO MY GRANDCHILDREN WITH ALL MY LOVE:

JACOB, PENELOPE, GRACE AND STANLEY

IN MEMORY OF BARRY CUTTELL

INTRODUCTION

Recently I turned 72 years of age. It crept up on me and I wish it hadn't. I think of my friends and suddenly realise that there are probably only half a dozen older than me and that is frightening. There is no escape from the march of Time: even one of my heroes, Bruce Springsteen, is 72 this year. Soon, every morning in bed, I will read the Obituaries in THE paper and if I am not there I can get up!

So before it's too late I needed to explain why another book and the influences on it of three parts of my life: The Great War, Camping Authuille (pronounced Oatwheel!) and Family and Friends.

I proudly claim to be a pure Londoner, cultural proof being that I can talk proper as a Southerner and am proud of it - I have a BARF, I LARF a lot, I cut the GRARSS not like these bloody northerners with their baaths and so on! I was born in Charing Cross hospital just over the road from the station and about 4 miles from Bow Bells and the more amusingly appropriate Bow Locks. You can't get more London than that!

I grew up in Brockley in what is now a suburb of London, postcode SE4, but was then in Kent, with my Dad, a librarian, my Mum a housewife who developed dementia at the age of 50 and my younger, brighter, more beautiful sister Ellen.

Also in this three storey Victorian house lived my Grandad and Grandma.

Although the Great War had been over for thirty-one years when I was born it has always fascinated me; both my grandfathers were veterans, a Royal Fusilier and a Royal Wiltshire Yeoman respectively and proud wearers of Squeak and Wilfred (the British War Medal and Victory Medal), medals familiar to me especially on Remembrance Sunday.

I passed my 11 plus and went to a prestigious 500 year old boys' Grammar school, much to everyone's delight except mine - I hated it. Most of the teachers were incompetent sadists or perverts - how seriously can you take a school where the head of PE had a wooden leg and his deputy flicked your bum with a wet towel as you went in and out of the shower!

When I was 12 my beloved Grandad died – the first broken heart of my life.

At 15 the Pick & Mix stall in Woollies in Lewisham became the object of my desires - I fell in love with a Saturday girl who was also a choirgirl, who was bright, worked hard at grammar school, loved Joan Baez, Bob Dylan and all that trendy liberal shit and went off to uni with stunning A level grades. I did none of these things so was left pining at home. Heartache prompted me to follow a year later to Leicester but the only college I could get into was a teacher training college; what the hell, I didn't want to be a bloody teacher, I just wanted to Pick & Mix – a decision soon found to be wrong as when I got there she'd found someone else and I was dead meat - second broken heart!

It's funny how insignificant events change your life: deeply indulged in my melancholia, one day I met Carol who was at uni in Leeds, 100 miles away. I decided to drive up and visit her. My second car was a scrapheap on wheels and I set off on a wet dark Friday night up the M1. After a while the weather was so bad I thought of turning round and going back;

I didn't, but what if I had? 52 years later all that matters is I did not.

There is no doubt that I have had a happy life, the reason is simple– friends and family, both of which I have been so fortunate with. The majority of my friends are teachers; schoolteachers are often mocked, mis-understood or looked upon as just plain boring. BOW LOCKS

There are at least eleven teachers and some pupils whom I have been privileged to have worked with and to call dear friends and boring they ain't. The monastic environment of education tries to turn pupils into potential adults but in the less formal atmosphere of school drama productions, for instance, they can become friends. Some of these, despite being taught by me, became and have remained friends and have done brilliantly well from becoming Head Boy/Head Girl to reaching the highest echelons in business, government etc.

We have lived in Saffron Walden for nearly 40 years and my interest in the Great War, nurtured on the names on the war memorial, came to be harvested in the purchase of a home in France at the centre of the Somme battlefields, just below the magnificent Thiepval Memorial with its 73000 names of the Missing.

Living for half of the year on a battlefield, one becomes familiar with the statistics, the detritus of war, the individual stories of ordinary people as well as the realisation that no-one, whether king or pauper, escaped the physical and psychological wounds of war. On her marriage in Westminster Abbey the Queen Mother placed her bouquet on the tomb of the Unknown Warrior in memory of her brother Fergus Bowes-Lyon killed at Loos in 1915 (a tradition repeated by all royal brides since). Herbert Asquith, Prime Minister, was often found sobbing in his study holding a photograph of his son, Raymond, killed on the Somme in 1916. Ferdinand Foch, the

French supreme allied commander in 1918, lost both his son and son-in-law in August 1914. Rudyard Kipling having 'pulled strings' to get his short-sighted son into the Irish Guards spent the rest of his life racked with guilt searching the battlefields of Flanders trying to find his son's remains. Vera Brittain lost her brother, her fiancé Roland Leighton and her two closest friends. The poet Siegfried Sassoon, 'Mad Jack,' recommended for the Victoria Cross but awarded the Military Cross, for the rest of his life would hide under the table whenever there was thunder.

The Great War has also been a catalyst for making new friends, both French and British, language being no problem when the universal language in "Oatwheel" is laughter.

The greatest cause of happiness has been my family from the very first moment that Ben, our eldest, refused to be born until it was my (and his Grandpa's birthday) to the arrival of my latest grandchild, Stanley- it has been a buzz!

Some years ago a dubious treat was bestowed upon me courtesy of a certain Mr Parkinson. An observation, nothing profound, but perhaps amusing: my prescription notes say, and I quote, ...side effects....persistent and abnormal erection of the penis. Well no such luck!

On that subtle note I think my feelings are best summed up in the words of Billy Connelly I'VE GOT PARKINSON'S DISEASE, I WISH HE'D F........G KEPT IT!

The bulk of the contents of this book is poetry and some prose inspired by a conflict over 100 years ago, some of it is inspired by friends and family. I could not resist the temptation to take a humorous, but I hope gentle stroll through Camping Authuille (forever Oatwheel) a cross between Clochemerle and Carry On Camping with its lovable owner the Renaissance Man our own JC.

The people I have thanked in my previous books continue to support and inspire me as do new friends Martine and Cyrille, Harry Taylor, with his vast knowledge which he is always willing to share; Gill and Malcolm and Judith, my translator.

I have taken the title for this book from the last line of a wonderful poem by Richard Molesworth Denys, a vivid example of the cream of society who were dubbed the 'Lost Generation", a doctor, pianist, painter, poet, writer, described as ....a man above all to know, and to be thankful for having known Perchance the coming night is full of stars.

POETRY

ANYONE FOR TENNIS?

There was no fear just an aching void.
He tried to conjure up her face,
To say goodbye, to say anything
For her presence to be with him.
Through his tears he saw
The limp torso of his friend Cliff.
Ever present flies already gathering,
Crimson, sticky stain growing on his tunic.

Fifty yards to the Turkish trenches
A field of corpses, the detritus of death
Piled one upon another.
Evidence of their failure:
Recumbent bodies of the heroic attackers
Ordered again and again to press forward
As the red and white flag had been glimpsed
Claiming triumph amidst the bloodied khaki.

With his destiny written there in front of him
He rose from the haven of the trench unafraid.
Blackness engulfed him,
His body flailing backwards
A scream of victory emblazoned in the air.

The charge at dawn on 7 August 1915 of the 8th and 10th Light Horse Regiments at the Nek in an area described by C E W Bean, as a 'strip the size of three tennis courts' where three waves and part of a fourth were cut down, most before they even got near the Turkish lines.

ARMISTICE

The last notes of the bugle faded, drifting
away on the gentle breeze.
A solitary plane leaf, red and gold in the
weak morning sun, spiralling in its fall.
Leaning on his stick, he tried to pull his
pain-wracked torso to attention,
An instinct from years of military discipline,
but the shrapnel deep
In his wasted leg protested, curtailing that idea.
Looking around the massed crowd,
the only sounds restrained sobbing,
He counted the widows, many clutching
children so close to them
As if fearful they would be snatched away.

She had been spared that pain;
the Hun bullet had seen to that
Smashing into his upper thigh, exiting through his groin.
His letter home had perhaps said too much;
she replied and had gone,
Ostensibly to a better position in London...
Another lonely leaf colourfully landed
on the empty pavement.

The subconscious ticking of the clock;
the two minutes almost gone.
Seemingly long but in truth so little time, for so many.
He instinctively stretched his leg; an involuntary cry of pain
Escaped his tightly drawn lips, no-one around him noticed,
Too deep in memories of their lost ones.

A slight murmur greeted the end of silence;
a cautious movement
As the throng edged towards the names they cherished.
Waiting, it would be easier when the crowd had thinned,
Remembering with frightening clarity how each had perished
A litany of comrades honoured in bronze
An obligation he must perform;
remembrance was all he had left.
Another leaf gently caressed his careworn
face on its autumnal fall.

A.R.P BLUES

There was a melancholy drizzle as he closed the front door
His last words, 'go to the shelter when they start,'
But would they listen, it wasn't very comfortable!
Not a soul was about; a sense of foreboding
Troubled him; the prospect of another night
When the autumn sky would rain death.
Retribution for the assault on enemy cities
The vengeful V2 silent murderers of men...and women
Oblivious to age or innocence.

Streets in a skeletal landscape,
Desolate, their dwellers gone to ground.
His task to ensure all was blacked out
Edwardian houses of the bourgeoisie;
Females, children and old men
No able-bodied men here, at some
Far-flung front they should be.
He'd done his bit, Arras on Easter Monday
No picnic, nearly thirty years ago!
His sons somewhere, both Desert Rats,
Only his wife and two daughters in the house.

These reflections were punctuated by
Explosions just two streets away,
Roads where they lived, fear gripped his soul
As he ran, blackout no more
Amidst the flaming ruins.
He was there, involuntarily he called out
The house had gone, broken furniture burning
Nothing left standing, no sign of life.

Falling to his knees he wept
Acrid smoke around him, fire-engine bells,
He must do his job, but as he stood
From the darkness, ethereal, ghost-like
He glimpsed three figures arms out-stretched
Running towards him and he knew
They had listened to him.

In memory of my dear Grandad, a Royal Fusilier in the Great War and an air-raid Warden in south-east London in the Second World War. This story is true.

BROTHERHOOD OF RIGHT

Seven more friends; men in love with peace
But willing to fight and die; to ensure the sanctity of Right.
So who better than a Poilu, albeit not a 'hairy one
Denis, a big man in every way, not a 'grognard**' he!
Never without a smile, ever willing to lead,
strong yet creative,
The heat of battle nothing to the heat of his beloved kitchen!

Mick, different as chalk and camembert. A hairy one – yes
'Grognard.' most definitely, a big man in a more rotund way.
He likes his beef rare and his women well-done,
Or is it the other way round.
It matters little, he believes in the
Brotherhood of Right and the universal language of laughter.

Polishing his rifle fastidiously next to him on the fire-step,
Jon, the eternal optimist, always ready
to see the best in everyone,
Even the Hun, the enemy, now that's going a bit too far!!
Fit as the proverbial fiddle, shy, quiet, the perfect comrade.

Waiting patiently in the shade of the finest
beer-gut on the Somme,
Estaminet maintained, it belongs to Neil, the mimic,
A volatile mix of Lowland Scot and Brixton Cockney
He's seen the world, been there, done it, broke it
Mended it – how do we know? He told us!
Kind-hearted, amusing, bullshit with courage.

Some espouse intellectuality and class, some have it naturally
Thus is Michael, 'a veray parfit gentil knight,'
The Queen's English, pure cut-glass accent, in short 'posh,'
But beware of judgements made on superficial criteria
Here is a man with backbone.

Here looms another gargantuan, Bruce.
The name itself suggests
Typical ANZAC qualities: bravery, irreverence,
Humour, larrikinism, mateship.
Add to this "Onward Christian Soldier,'
and we have our man.

Malcolm
Intellect and Humour. Compassion and courage
Are qualities priceless individually, but in one rare indeed.
A privilege to share a trench
At least we'll die laughing Malc!

** *Grognard - veteran soldier, specifically an old grenadier of
the Imperial Guard (Grenadiers à pied de la Garde Impériale);
an old complaining soldier*

*A further flight of fancy of Seven more for the Band of
Brothers, as diverse a crew as could be imagined. Dear friends
who would all fulfil Alexander the Great's words - Remember
upon the conduct of each depends the fate of all.*

CARPE DIEM (SEIZE THE DAY)
Written on July 1st 2020,

Waking with a start, wedged between the elderly Corporal
Snoring stentoriously and the shy waif-like
lad from Lewisham.
To his surprise he had slept despite sitting
on an insensitive petrol can,
The noise, the danger, but most of all the fear.

Dawn was breaking, the breeze from the east propelling a few
Fleecy clouds in an azure firmament where
the sun infused some early warmth
Enhanced by the welcome arrival of a tot of rum
A morning more suited for a picnic than battle, he mused!

Glancing at his watch showed a minute
or two before 6.30 a.m zero-hour.
Attempts to inform his comrades were drowned
in a gigantic roar

As the guns erupted, beginning
the hour- long bombardment of
'Fortress Gommecourt Wood'

To wait amidst such mayhem was draining,
Fighting hysteria and an overwhelming urge to flee,
Pandemonium ruled, the noise mind-numbing.
Another glance 7.30.
The first wave was on top ready.
Knowing he was next he scrambled through
the battered trench
All that mattered was now, the present, the attack,
the signal to "seize the day."

FORD (SIT UP & BEG) POP

The long slow slope allowed me to pull in front of the
Lugubrious lorry straining up the hill just as
The heavens opened, and dusk like a curtain fell.
In other circumstances the fact that
The more you pushed the accelerator down,
The slower the wipers went, eventually stopping,
Would have been cause for hilarity, but today only trepidation.
As I squeezed the old heap back in front of the lorry he
Irritably flashed, scaring me shitless with his horn.

There are times in life when a simple decision can affect
Everything and everybody in one's existence to come.
Unaware this was my whole being's defining moment,
I examined the facts - driving rain, pitch black.
I could turn round, go back, no loss of face.
Alone in my ancient vehicle -one hundred miles
to go, for what?
A pretty girl, now let's be honest a VERY pretty girl
Whom, I had met a couple of times, who quite frankly,
But understandably,

HAD TAKEN NO NOTICE OF ME

BUT Some powerful deity must have been
amused by my quandary,
Looking forward to some amusement at
my innocent expense.
Eager to see if the old banger was up to it,
I decided to carry on, especially as she was so pretty.
A fair few more doubts were aired that journey,
But harbour was safely reached and my life began in earnest.
I fell in love with Carol, immediately, uniquely,
coincidentally, calling
Her Carrie, the preferred name of her beloved
Grandmother Caroline.

It is now fifty years ago that we got engaged
on my 21st birthday.
During those early years we needed nothing but one another.
No need for children or a house, or updated car.
Until one day it seemed the appropriate thing to do.
We have been blessed with three lovely children, friends now.
Their looks and brains from their beautiful mother.
Their faults, though few in number, from me!

LOVE IS A MANY-SPLENDORED THING.

One day my Ford Pop was taken to a Chinaman for repair.
It was never seen again nor was the Chinaman!
Some years later I received a speeding ticket through the post.
Speeding, you must be 'avin a larf!!

THANK YOU VXU 265

We travelled and learnt and loved and still she is soooo pretty!!
Je t'aime

FUTURE OF A VAD

One week he had been in her care and now he was gone.
His young, bronzed body looked perfect lying on the stretcher
But for the huge gash across his stomach where the bullet had
  Almost cut him in half; the vivid scarlet gore on the sheets
Where the omnipresent flies gathered to feast and wallow.

Through tears she gently cleaned his frame
Wiping the dried sweat, the encrusted blood.
Two years ago her life was planned: school,
    university, marriage, children.
She pursued a life of isolated middle-class comfort.
    An only child
Her limited knowledge of men gained from a humourless
Father and her doting mother's younger brother,
An Anglican cleric cocooned in the depths of
    bucolic Herefordshire.

Then arrived THE GREAT WAR and
life changed in every way.
Study of the Crimea became her obsession and
under the influence of a
Nightingale in Scutari and to her parents'
horror and disbelief
She became a VAD and so began
A voyage from innocence to experience,
Cosseted rural Kent to front-line field hospital via
The Bull-Ring in Etaples and a hospital ship in Malta.

Gently dabbing his boyish face, the lids never to open again
On those eyes of deep azure blue
Her task coming to a close, the early evening drawing in,
She looked again at the object of her reverie.
A pallor was creeping over him,
the insidious evidence of death
Fading from the world of Man to the domain of the maggot
Where the next day a newly-dug trench would
receive six bodies.

Deep in her thoughts, a solitary tear rolled down her cheek
Causing her to regain her composure.
On the stretcher her bronzed Adonis with the blue eyes lay
Blissfully unaware of the impact he had had in death
On the future of a VAD.

Dedicated to my favourite 'Nursie,' Yorkshire's finest,
Jo 'Josephine, (Not tonight)' Beddows

THE HARLEM HELLFIGHTERS

Faces that stare at you, haunted, crushed, lacking in certainty,
All in uniform, but most of all BLACK.
A photo taken on board a ship home-bound,
Mindful of those they left behind enriching the
soil of Mother France,
Kept apart from fright-eyed white conscripts,
Tasked to save the free world from the prejudice of the Hun
But not allowed to fight, only to labour and die.

BLACK RATTLERS

Given second-rate weapons, inferior uniforms.
"Blacks can't fight," spat the Kentucky Colonel
Over his bourbon as they marched by.
"You should see us Saturday night in Harlem," quipped Joe.
Ironic smiles creased their joyous faces.
Fate took pity, France was bleeding dry.
They knew how to fight, fight and die with elan.

Inspired by La Fayette the poilus welcomed
Their presence where Death commanded,
181 days in combat, the proof in every cemetery.

MEN OF BRONZE

They did not seek any other reward but
To return home to loved ones, friends, to safety.
After two years of duty done
Memories left deep in the rolling fields
Where the black man and his ami, le poilu,
Stitched up the Argonne!
Rewarded by a medal, see they wear it, in the photo -
The Croix -de-Guerre,
"Is that Frog for cannot fight," wise-cracked Joe.

Home bound now, contemplative
Surely it would be different, surely?
But medals meant nothing
Buddies left behind for a world unchanged
Nothing to smile about
All that endures is comradeship.

DON'T TREAD ON ME,
GOD DAMN. LET'S GO

Harlem Hellfighters, 369th Infantry Regiment, originally 15th New York (Coloured) Infantry Regiment.
   Black troops were deemed second-class and only fit for labouring. They were issued with sub-standard equipment and uniforms. French losses were so great that black troops were used to fill the gaps. So successful were they that the French government decorated the entire unit with the Croix de Guerre, its highest award for bravery, as well as 170 additional individual medals for valour.

JUST ANOTHER DAY!

Dark descended, damp, cold, deadly,
Clinging like a shroud, the world a crypt.
Visions of home filled his mind, memories, events,
Happier times which he futilely tried to forget.
Call this daylight! At home lamps would be lit all day,
Here he peered into the gloom
Till his eyes ached, rewarded by nothing more than
The occasional flicker of a match.
A dilatory dog barked behind the enemy lines.
A sudden strident snore escaped from the dormant figure
Next to him, causing him to jump involuntarily.
Jim was always snoring, whatever the risk.
Shaking him he only received a mouthful of Cockney abuse
As he turned to resume his slumber.
So much for saving his mate's life!
Contemplating the floor of the trench,
Duckboards covered with sludge
Which filled his already sodden boots,

Seeping up his puttees to the knees,
He felt for the first time the bitter cold,
Noticed his blue hands soldered with cold to his rifle.

Grimly smiling to himself, so far Jim had escaped punishment,
But one day.... Dismissing that as too much to contemplate
His only bright thought was that the Hun would not
Leave the sanctuary of his cosy trenches tonight
So all he had to worry about was snipers and 5.9s
And with luck he might cop a Blighty one
Or better still Jim might!
Two hours to relief
JUST ANOTHER DAY

LAST CHANCE

Pain woke him from the depths of darkness,
The driving rain battering the canvas,
Overwhelming the moans, the cries of pain.
Through it all a voice, soft but familiar,
Calling him, Robert, Robert!

The first voice he had ever heard, his mother.
Plaintive, yet comforting, evoking memories of childhood.
Christened Bob she only called him Robert
when he had been naughty.
He remembered this was rare, he was her favourite.
Perpetually pregnant he had witnessed
four brothers and sisters die.
In the flickering candlelight, the nurse wrapped
another cloak,
Around her shoulders as outside the storm
took no prisoners.

When war came, encouraged by his Cockney father,
he had eagerly joined
A London regiment, feeling more at home than
with the local Essex yokels!
October saw him wondering if the landing
on the sandy shores at Suvla Bay
Would be like the childhood charabanc trips to Southend.
Far from it, the heat even so late in the year, unbearable,
Johnny Turk peppering the crowded beaches from the hills,
You didn't have that at Leigh-on-Sea!
It was as they launched an attack across the Salt Lake,
Slow-moving black dots of humanity on a white surface,
That a Turkish bullet ripped into his stomach.

A Red Cross tent on Lemnos was where
Fate deemed he should die,
But not before a journey through the barriers of pain
Ending where angelic nurses could only ease his passing.
Shivering. despite the extra cloak, shielding the candle from
the draught,
The nurse patrolled between the beds.
As she passed, he called out trying to catch her hand,
But the wind and flapping canvas were all she heard as she sat
again at her post.

Despair gripped him and pain wracked his slender frame,
He was alone and afraid,
The gloom engulfing him seemed impenetrable,
But a plaintive voice, a dim light slowly defined,
Growing closer, brighter and the voice soothing and familiar.
Mother, her hands outstretched coming towards him smiling,
Behind her, arms linked, George, Gertrude, John and Alice
And he was at peace.

LATTICE OF DEATH

Objective, the Sugar Loaf, a concrete bastion of
Machine guns. Defenders, expectant, resolute
Spitting death over favourable ground.
Bullets, a lattice of death, decimating the innocence
Of untried digger soldiers......and a few Brits
Buried in haphazard communal graves!
The worst day in Australian military history'

GONE .... BUT ALS0 FORGOTTEN

Forgotten for ninety-years, the knowledge
Of its existence fades, just a Flanders' field
Until a man with a mission needs to discover,
Persuades the use of DNA, TV ads
Revealing fresh trails, red tape removed
Warriors identified, but no Brits
only Australian

FREEZING FLANDERS

On a winter's morning, frosted Flanders.
First burials, a new cemetery, Pheasant Wood.
A continuous process to identify the lost digger soldiers......
and a few Brits

So the cemetery grows, the names are found
Families claim their lost past,
Discovered, inscriptions chosen
Because they're diggers!
Sadly Brits made no effort, so no Brits identified.

HOT AS HELL

Summer comes, a chosen day to celebrate
The "finding of the lost"
In the presence of the great, the good.
Villagers attired in their Sunday best,
Hot as hell, audience fainting in droves.
Symbolic moment to remain in the memory:
Marching through the leafy local lanes
Behind a flag-draped British gun carriage,
The lady Governor-General of Australia
And the heir to the throne, Charles, later
Impressively quoting Australia's greatest war poet.

THE GREAT DISGRACE

The opening is not the end,
Every new find still loved, honoured, remembered,
Pride in the sacrifice, a debt owing
An obligation paid
But only if Australiian

But no Brit because

WE CANNOT BE BOTHERED

Fromelles, 19th July 1916, two infantry divisions attacked the notorious "Sugar Loaf".

The action turned into a bloody catastrophe and remains the worst day in Australian military history.

Completed in July 2010, Fromelles (Pheasant Wood) Military Cemetery is the first new war cemetery to be built by the CWGC in fifty years.

In Australia, a media campaign to identify as many casualties as possible has been very successful.

No such campaign has taken place in the UK and the results speak for themselves. The cemetery contains a total of 250 Australian and British soldiers. 225 are Australians, of which 59 are unidentified, 2 are unidentified British soldiers and 23 are entirely unidentified Commonwealth soldiers.

The 250 were recovered in 2009 from a number of mass graves located behind nearby Pheasant Wood.

M LE MAIRE, REGIS SCHOONHEERE

From time immemorial the rivers Ancre and
Somme have seduced the British.
The English Warrior-King, Henry V,
crossed the wintry Somme to Azincourt
Where English bowmen destroyed the knights
of Charles d'Albret.
From enemy to friend, poilu and Tommy
stand shoulder to shoulder
To quell the Hun invaders.

The Military Cemetery where over 400 Tommies
Lie in the earth of Mother France and
The village Memorial with the sacred names of its children
who died for Freedom.

Today the link remains with Camping Bellevue
where les Anglais return to Remember.
Fought over until the ways of peace eventually prevail,
Authuille has for the last twenty years been led
by a true man of the Somme,
Proud of the past he never fails to decorate the
War Memorial,
To don the republican sash; to welcome
the inquisitive pilgrim.

Authuille, much beloved by home-sick Great War writers.
Reminiscent of bucolic southern Blighty,
Historically its importance outweighs its size.
A mayor comfortable with royalty, statesmen,
pomp and circumstance
To show the village, his village, in all its glory.

The time has come to spend more moments
with the grandchildren,
To perfect those arrow straight furrows
in the plot behind his house,
To welcome every new group of English travellers,
To look around him to see the evidence of
his patriotic devotion.

M LE MAIRE, REGIS SCHOONHEERE

Pour toujours les rivières d'Ancre et de la
Somme ont été séduit par les Anglais.
Le Roi Henri V- guerrier anglais a traversé la
Somme hivernale jusqu'à Azincourt
Où les archers anglais ont détruit les chevaliers
de Charles d'Albret.
De l'ennemi à l'ami, poilu et Tommy débout épaule à épaule
Pour calmer le Hun, les envahisseurs.

La cimitière militaire où plus de 400Tommies
se reposent sous la terre de la Mère France
Et Le monument commémoratif avec des noms
sacrés de ses enfants morts pour la Libérté
Au'jourd'hui le lien existe toujours avec le Camping Bellevue
Où les Anglais reviennent pour se souvenir.

On se battait, jusqu'à ce qu' à la fin les chemins
de la paix triomphent
Pendant vingt ans Authuille a été dirigée par un
vrai homme de la Somme
Fier du passé, il n'échoue jamais à décorer
le monument commémoratif,
Ou à porter la ceinture républicaine: à accueillir
le pèlerin curieux.

Authuille, admirée par des nostalgiques grands
écrivains de la Grande Guerre,
Qui évoque Blighty bucolique du sud
Son importance historique dépasse sa taille
Un maire à l'aise avec la royauté, les hommes d'état,
la pompe at la circonstance
Et à montrer le village, son village, en toute sa gloire.

Et maintenant, l'heure est arrivée à passer
plus de moments avec des petits enfants
Pour perfectionner ces sillons droits comme
une flèche sur le terrain derrière sa maison
A recevoir chaque groupe de pèlerins anglais
Et à voir tout autour de lui l'évidence de son
dévouement patriotique.

Made oop north – and proud of it!!

Isolated boy among a gaggle of girls

Career determined as dad before.

He decides to be different

Away from his roots – guardian of our skies

Enters the "mob"– air force to me and you!

Looks very dapper in uniform!

But destiny intervenes

In spite of being "dahn south"

Romances and wins Essex's finest

New wife, new daughter to add to the clan

Individuality – still in shorts in winter, sans teeth!

Everything we love – our Mick!

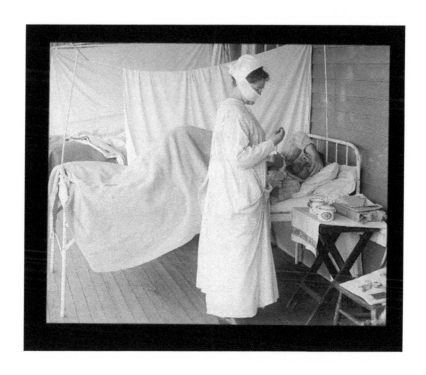

OCTOBER IS THE CRUELLEST MONTH

September 1918. The end near or so we were told,
One last attack; the Hun was on the run.
He had not felt the hot shard rip through his thigh.
Tying a belt around the oozing wound,
The blood seeping, soaking his sock, his boot.
The interminable trudge to the CCS hastened by
Fear of losing too much blood, or a well-judged enemy shell.

Sunshine filtered through the thin gauze curtain
Flooding the crumpled bed where he lay.
Since reaching sanctuary and the recognition he was safe,
A sense of complacent triumph had regularly
awakened him,
The pain of the wound forgotten,
no longer the stench of decay,

Solace of a war ended, a Blighty One,
captured at the perfect moment,
A new life beckoned.

Today however things were different,
a feeling of fever, nausea, chill.
Shivers wracked him as he saw his neighbour's
empty bed.
Silently a nurse entered taking his temperature,
writing it down
With a sense of doom as she drew the
curtains around his bed,
A gentle smile upon her saintly face,
An imperceptible touch of her cool fingers across his brow....
and he knew!

The 1918 influenza pandemic, colloquially known as Spanish flu, was unusually deadly. It infected 500 million people around the world, and resulted in the deaths of 50 to 100 million (three to five percent of the world's population), making it one of the deadliest natural disasters in human history.

ON THE WINGS OF THE WIND

In the sanctity of the cockpit.
Alone with the steady hymn of the gently vibrating engine,
Filled with the pungent smell of oil,
Guilt feelings still preyed on his soul.
Like his brother he had rebelled against the
Friends' teachings which they had followed since birth,
A decision that had caused his father much anguish.

It was now two years since the decision was made.
He was a seasoned soldier, wounded once,
Sent for officer training with the RFC.
He knew he had taken the right course
So why did it still trouble him?

Deep in thought, the sudden cessation of his engine
Shocked him back to the world of here and now.
The gentle descent as in a silent void,
All was serene, he was alone with God.

He felt no fear, confident in his skill.
He was in control, safety 500 feet below,
Just needing to turn towards the airfield.
As he did, he felt the control no longer his,
The gentle descent spiralled into a fall,
Plummeting earthwards.
In that fleeting moment he heard his father's voice,
'He makes the clouds his chariot,
He rides on the wings of the wind.'

Sensing the nearness of his God
He felt at peace
As the funeral pyre engulfed him.

In memory of Stephen Walker who came from a strict Quaker family. His father became headmaster of the Friends School Saffron Walden. Despite his religious beliefs he and one of his brothers served.

PACKAGE

The package arrived swathed in brown,
too big for the ancient letterbox,
A postman eager to thrust it in her supplicant arms.
Bemused for a moment till she read 'from the French frontier.'
Four short words that aroused the pain she thought had gone,
Re-awakened her loneliness and sorrow,
leaving her empty, sick, lost.

He had been a soldier for eleven years intent on going far,
Rising through the ranks, educating himself
so he could others.
Hers was love at first sight, not just the uniform
But the smile ever present, whatever the circumstance.
She recalled his constant axiom:
"A soldier's a man, his life but a span."
His pride in his profession knew no limits,
Even when a painful wound led to a posting in Egypt
Where dysentery felled him and frustration ruled his recovery.

France beckoned again, but was there a sense of doom
In his au revoir to his wife as he held his 'bairn' aloft?
Joining his battalion near Vendegies Wood,

Advancing over open country,
Fighting all the way, driving the enemy before them,
In the best traditions of the Battalion, he was killed;
He had been back a mere eleven days.

Tearfully, carefully, she carried the parcel to the table
A package that, with memories, was all that was left of him.
Opening it carefully, avoiding tearing the grubby wrapping,
It became brutally apparent much was not there,
stolen, or lost.
She neither knew, nor cared, all that mattered was it had gone
And with it her tangible remembrances of her soldier.

In memory of Lieutenant Alfred John WYATT 1st. attached 8th. Cameronians (Scottish Rifles), killed in action October 23rd. 1918, aged 32. Buried in Highland Cemetery, Le Cateau, France, Plot 8 Row E Grave 7.

The last officer from Saffron Walden to die in the Great War.

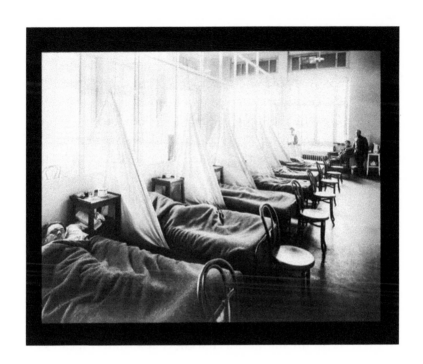

PESTILENCE

It had been the flies, feasting on the bloated corpses
Then upon the food you ate, impossible to get to your mouth
Before it became a crunchy carpet of greenbottles.
Then dysentery, memories of Herr Bailey's salivating delight
In German the literal translation, a favourite, 'durch wasser.'
The arrival of cold weather slowed the descent into oblivion
But for six weeks getting weaker by the day until
The ticket to Blighty, westward to recovery and hope.

Daily the transport parallel to an azure hazy shore
A perception of white chalk houses, clean, pristine
A pastoral poem echoing in his mind:
'I to the hills will lift mine eyes,'
Delight of a boiled egg in Gibraltar!

Getting stronger, the nightmare fading, hope replacing fear.
Finally, a cold and foggy land of my mothers,
Gently transferred to a hospital bed.
Outside the smog lived up to its reputation
Pea soup was never so green, so acrid, but so welcome,
He knew that he had triumphed.

As he lay looking out on a leaden sky, clouds racing,
Squally rain showers beating upon the glass,
He sensed it wasn't like last time, there
was no glimmer of hope,
No light at the end of the recovery tunnel.
He knew all his plans and dreams were worthless,
The war was over, he had survived
But fate had not finished with him.
In his feverish dreams all was darkness in a subterranean sap.

He had avoided shot and shell, praying without conviction,
For relief, a future, but his entreaties had fallen
On barren ground and all was lost.
Fate had dealt him a losing hand -
There was no rhyme nor reason why,
But as dusk fell outside, a sense of stoical calm
Descended upon him as he drifted towards
The end, a realisation that no matter what
He had done his duty and was content.

The Great War claimed an estimated 16 million lives. The influenza epidemic that swept the world in 1918 killed an estimated 50 million people. One fifth of the world's population was attacked by this deadly virus. Within months, it had killed more people than any other illness in recorded history many had been survivors of the war, this poem is dedicated to them.

POET'S CORNER

Behind the curtain of smoke, half-hidden
in the insignificance of shadow, he felt content, safe.
For a brief time behind the line, Death, the perpetual shadow,
was forgotten until a new cull, another bitter harvest.
For now he was happy dozing, drowsily
observing through the smoke.

His comrades, new friends, accepted he was different.
Suspicious at first, he had intrigued them
until the chance finding of a notebook had
confirmed everything.
Eager to ridicule, to bully, they found instead poems,
which stilled their mocking laughter, fed their curiosity.
His ability to create laughter, tears, to put in
words their feelings
until the day came when the bully sheepishly asked for one
to send home to secure his love.

The corner became his sanctuary, noise did not distract him;
he did not drink much but he seldom needed any,
he just watched and wrote.

His letters home said little.
Three sisters and a mother would not approve
of the flirtatious waitresses,
tight-roping a tenuous path between promiscuity
and mock virginity.
He did not mind this game played out before him
but coarse words adopted by the girls offended
his sense of feminine propriety.
He smiled at the irony, comely girls flirting naively
attracted him by their precocity.
He almost persuaded himself that his three sisters ought
to have helped him understand women, but they had not.
Madam reminded him of his mother.
Perhaps the absence of a father intensified his feelings,
but he was uncomfortable with his attraction,
it felt more than filial.

He marvelled how things had changed;
how different he was.
He had become a good soldier, never complaining,
always a smile.
No longer embarrassed when another beer mysteriously
found its way onto his table.
Drinking a little more, watching the antics of his friends,
indulged in because there was no tomorrow,
only the promised Big Push.
Everything was written down: dreams of home,
the warmth, comfort.
The aroma of women seduced him to compose
mildly erotic verse.

To his surprise he was asked to write a last letter,
followed by more.
It troubled him, how many could he write,
it forced him to think of his mortality.
He could only create if words came from the heart.
War had destroyed his adolescence.
Life he had little experience of,
but he was aware of the pain of Madam
seeing a broken heart in every action,
a serene sadness in her smile.
Her husband was missing near Verdun.
He wanted to show her he knew, he understood,
to hold her close.
Many men in the village desired her -
a young woman with the café, with little chance of
Gerard returning.
His notebook full of attempts to explain his desire
in a different language.
Words, for him, more than a confession of erotic guilt
but it was impossible,
he could only show his sympathy by sharing his smile
as she served the beer carried in glasses resting
on her broken heart.

The young soldier whose eyes followed
her every movement
from the corner intrigued her, his smile charmed her and
in the sanctity of her room
the emptiness of her bed seemed ever more
cold and lonely.
Tomorrow, one day, he would leave, never return
to watch her across the floor, to share their
enigmatic smiles.

As in a trance, he closed the notebook,
putting it in his breast pocket, on the heart side.
Rising from the chair in the smoke-filled corner
his pre-occupied comrades called for him to stay.
Their entreaties caused her to look up and her eyes met his.
As if in slow-motion, as he passed he bent and gently,
oh so gently kissed her and he was gone.
On her powdered face the smile faded,
a solitary tear running down her soft rouged cheek
as the Angel of Death quietly closed the door.

RED, WHITE & GREEN

Looking at his watch, 06.20,
The words, "They'll just be about to start,,,,,,,"
Drowned in the gigantic roar
Of the deafening British guns.

Crouching deep in the tumbling trench,
Smaller shells shrill above their heads,
An hour of hell to wait.
Afraid yet eager to go over the top
Free from the prison of the claustrophobic trench,
Free from the raucous shell fire,
Free to walk across No Man's Land.

As if waking suddenly from a nightmare
The time had arrived.
Smoke obscured the future,
Shell-holes pitted the way,
Bodies dotted the landscape,
Ladders smashed or used as stretchers.
Amidst screams of pain

The way to the German lines was open,
A way through the white of the smoke
The grass still green
But both dominated by the
Red of the shrapnel and shockingly...the blood

THE ARROW

There was no doubt which way it pointed,
Its certainty gave a sense of security, of safety,
Preparation in the event of invasion
From the east towards front-line Essex.
One hundred years later a little shabby,
Never needed, unique, it still defines the way.
Essex had been his practice zone
The feared Zeppelin raids, 'baby killers'
Dealing silent death from the skies.
Indiscriminate bombardment from the sea
Easy pickings, not too far to come
To 'soften up' and then to invade?

The steadfast arrow became the symbol of a strategy
To counter this fear, another weapon
In the master plan containing
Instructions to kill all livestock, to get rid

Of all alcohol removing the excuse
For drunken invaders to
Replicate the atrocities of Belgium!
Then to flee due east IF he came.
Perhaps the realisation that it was a groundless fear;
After all the genius of Napoleon had failed
What chance Bill the crippled Kaiser!

The arrow, another tool from the quiver of defiance,
Was superfluous and all but forgotten.
Just one neglected, un-noticed symbol
Of a will to survive; to negate the powers of evil,
Its message as unequivocal,
As recognisable as the day it appeared.

*These and many similar arrows were painted to direct
non-combatants inland across country avoiding
main roads to facilitate the movement of troops in the
event of a successful landing by the Germans on the
East Coast 1914-1918.
This is one of very few known arrows still surviving.*

THE COMING NIGHT IS FULL OF STARS

Sun shivered on the dust motes streaming
through the nave window.
Victorian stained glass, little subtlety, garish colours
Worthy of any child's painting pot.
Entrenched in their belief in God, their place
in the scheme of things.

Thoughts interrupted by the entry of the coffin, my Mother's,
Provoked stirrings of guilt that my mind
had been preoccupied.
Feeling the need to explain to myself I felt tears close.

As the service unravelled, I found myself again elsewhere.
Beneath the west window hung a large
polished memorial brass
Reflecting, mirror-like, the mourning throng.
But more hypnotic for me, almost inducing a cry of delight,

Was that the name upon it was one of the war poets
Richard Molesworth Denys.

Outside the rites of passage of my mother
Traced a familiar route.
In retrospect I live with an inner guilt that Mum
Seemed less important than a dead poet,
She had been ill, death surely a release.
I feel now that his presence helped me through
A distressing day, his words expressing a symbol of hope,
A remembrance of love and the promise
That the coming night would be full of stars.

THE GUARDIAN

Eyes firmly fixed on the surrounding battlefields
Where so many still lie, hidden by Nature,
untouched by Time,
Never forgotten, guarded by the heart and
soul of Mother France.
At the heart of the village stands a living symbol of patriotism
Seen every day by every resident, a template
For what is right, what matters.
Thirteen names, many still familiar,
some at one with the fields of
Verdun, of Artois, the Somme, one at the Dardanelles.
A few returned, disabled, one seeking release,
Dragged from the depths of the mill race on the Ancre.

Four long years of parting left widows, a life of loneliness,
Children whose father was a stranger or an empty void.
A kind of normality returned but a need to know Why.

To assuage the grief a memorial was proposed,
Resplendent with thirteen names in the centre of the village
Surmounted by the head and shoulders of a poilu, a grognard.
Rumour was that as money was short,
No need for a full statue,
The important attributes of courage, brains and loyalty
Were abundant in the armless figure!!
La Patrie approved.

On a Spring day in 1922 watched by every villager,
Decorated by la Tricolor and wreaths of cornflowers,
A simple column that symbolises so much.
The sounds of la Marseillaise floated on the
breeze across the valley
Accompanied by a lonely sob.

For over one hundred years of war, occupation and peace
Le poilu has, unchanged and unchanging,
been Guardian for the village
Remembering les enfants d'Authuille morts pour la France.

LE GARDIEN

Des yeux fixés sur les environs des champs de bataille
Où beaucoup se couchent encore, cachés par la
Nature, jamais touchés par le Temps
Jamais oubliés, protégés par le cœur et
l'âme de la Mère France
Au cœur du village, il y a un symbole vivant du patriotisme
Vu chaque jour par chaque résident
Un modèle
De ce qui est juste et de ce qui importe
Treize noms, beaucoup encore connus,
quelques uns unis avec les champs
De Verdun, d'Artois, de la Somme, un aux Dardenelles
Certains sont revenus, infirmes, un qui cherchait la liberté
Tiré des profondeurs de la course du moulin sur l'Ancre.

Quatre années longues de la séparation ont
laissé des veuves, une vie de solitude

Un père d'enfants qui était un étranger ou un abîme vide
Un type de normalité est retourné mais avec
besoin de savoir pourquoi
Pour apaiser le chagrin on a proposé un mémorial
Magnifique avec treize noms au centre du village
Surmonté par la tête et les épaules d'un poilu, d'un grognard
On disait que l'argent manquait
Alors, pas besoin d'une statue complète
Les attributs importants du courage, d'intelligence,
et de la fidélité
Etaient abondants en forme de figure sans bras !
La patrie a approuvé.

Un jour de printemps en 1922 regardée par chaque villageois
Décorée par le tricolore et les guirlandes de bleuets
Une simple colonne qui symbolise tellement
Des sons de la Marseillaise ont flottés sur la brise à travers la
vallée, accompagnés d'un sanglot solitaire
Pendant plus de cent années de guerre, de l'occupation et de
la paix le poilu n'a pas changé, toujours constant, a été le
gardien du village se souvenant toujours des enfants
d'Authille morts pour la France.

THE OLD CONTEMPTIBLE

On my 70th birthday my son, Ben, wrote me this poem. If imitation is the sincerest form of flattery i.e one imitates someone else because one admires that person or values what that person is doing, I could not have received a more wonderful present.

The Field Marshall looks out at his troops
and surveys the scene.
As always they are ready, well trained by their
commander. His vast experience
passed down from one soldier to the next.
The eldest, his Captain, a fiery red head, athletic and
gung-ho, who always leads by
example, never willing to send his men to do
something he would not do himself.
The next, his lieutenant, the thoughtful one,
strategic in his approach, ever careful to
ensure the men are looked after.

His third, the youngest, yet wise beyond her years,
this reflected in her rank.
Intrepid without doubt, a risk taker,
but securely in control of her own destiny.
All of his officers willing and eager to please,
grateful for the kindness and care he
has shown them.
Loyalty engrained from a young age, founded on
their leader's wealth of knowledge.
Ever ready to do battle, to stand shoulder to
shoulder with the man they call 'Dad'.
Small in stature, Napoleonic in his wisdom,
he inspires respect from those he meets.
A passionate man, loving husband and devoted father.
His service record exemplary.
His battalion of 'pals' have been there throughout,
offering him council when needed.
Finally, his General, always by his side, his rock.
His voice of reason, ever ready to do her duty.
Without her, his climbing up the ranks, his life
may have been very different.
All of his achievements shared with his comrade,
through thick and thin, until the bitter end.
His inspection is finalised, his hard work rewarded.
For him, he knows that his job so
far has been a success.
The thunder of battle echoes in the distance,
and the promise he made many years
runs through his mind
His oath to protect his men, to fight for their
future burns as strongly today as it did
all those years ago.
Despite his ageing years and weary body his fight remains.
For honour, for freedom, for love.
Always for love.

TWO IS NOT ENOUGH

Suddenly two is not enough.
The cocoon of love has not faded
But there is an excess to share,
a whole new adventure to explore
Through the unknown territory of a new being,
flesh of our flesh.
Character an unknown amalgam of us with
Grandma's ginger hair!
Three weeks late he decides to appear on his father's birthday.
Not content with that it is also his Grandad's.
Is this a prophetic sign?
From squeezing soiled nappies to
A techni-coloured dreamcoat on the escalator of life,
Fulfilling parents' hopes and dreams both on and off the field:
A son to be proud of.

Avoiding the 'only child' syndrome was easy.
The lessons learnt with the first-born seemed simple enough
Confident in our skills, it was a surprise that
he could be so different.

But wait.... only in certain ways, no ginger hair for one!
But an abundance of humour; a boundless generosity
Collected in a new life on the stamp hinge of existence
Fulfilling hopes and dreams that we never knew we had!
From assuming a role to a love of the theatrical grand gesture
On a chosen path built of the same foundations
Leading to the same result:
A son to be proud of.

Two is a comforting round number but Fate disagreed.
It was decided to examine the skills of parenting on more
testing ground -
A girl! Ginger made a re-appearance with its added spice.
It was soon apparent one did not mess with this
independent spirit
A powerful commitment to doing what is right;
Self-belief that brooks no interference,
an innate courage needed
To travel half-way across the world in the
quest to broaden the mind,
An ingredient to be found in large measures in:
A daughter to be proud of.

The future unknown as another layer appears
Another melange of looks, another dip in the gene pool.
Confident that from the base we are so proud of,
Where the finest ingredients result in la crème de la crème,
A banquet will be served - the future is assured.

WHAT YOU SEE IS NOT WHAT YOU GET

Suddenly our quiet middle-class suburban haven
Became infiltrated by tattoos, piercings and ponytails,
Second hand car parts, mainly Jonny Foreigners,
littered the garden,
Garden! It was rumoured that it had become
An Engine Valhalla.

Behind the twitching lace, rumour upon rumour
Grew on Fertile ground for prejudice.
A scout went out equipped with poppies
Searching for final proof of depravity,
revolutionary behaviour
Expecting a refusal to buy.
The dye was cast.

Surprise, nay shock, greeted the scout -
Polite, well--spoken eager to support

Albeit a fully-paid up member of the SBS
The Scruffy Bugger Society.

Time passes and a deep friendship develops
As strong as any forged before.
Beneath the SBS is a man to look up to.
Not without fault, but loving, loyal, brave and practical
Helping old ladies across roads
Even when they don't want to!

Finally, the last hurrah,
Romance blossoms between our tattooed hero
And a daughter of fire who knows her mind,
Who saw long before the other bigots took on board
That you should not judge what is unseen
By external trappings!

Love ya Jason, or is it Gaston!

ZOUAVE

An armoire, unused, grubby, splendid in its ordinariness,
Harbouring the biggest spiders and who knows what more,
Had stood for years before he was born,
Stood ignored, until one day passing, its door open,
It was as if every colour, illuminated the gloom.
Clothes, old maybe, but enigmatic, mysterious, comic even,
Baggy, blue trousers, short sleeved silk jacket and hat.
Childlike he took the camphor smelling livery.

As he dressed a chuckle caused him to turn.
His father, eager to tell of their hidden existence,
Memories softened by over forty years,
But still a painful reminder of Prussian power.
No subtlety of field-grey or khaki;

A statement of victory not defeat.
Time to renew the struggle with flair,
A new generation with their quick drill
Short sleeves showing sturdy forearms
Manifestations of their strength.

The Zouave mantle thus became the son's,
More than a uniform, a statement of chivalric class.
Not mere cloth but silk with buttons gold and shiny
Flamboyant beneath a fez, garish but individual.
Recruits flocked to join, nations to copy,
Not just north African berbers, but all
Seduced, hypnotized.

There is no romance in war, even less in death.
The rolling hills of the Aisne and Marne,
The unsullied backdrop to the gaudy advances,
To the enemy positions extrovert in their courage,
Their blood-logged elan.

PROSE

MUSINGS FROM "OATWHEEL"

Authuille is a small French village located in <u>the department of the Somme</u> and the <u>Hauts-de-France</u> region (formerly Picardy). One hundred and sixty-seven people live in the village, which is four kms from Albert, the main town in the area. But for the Great War, Authuille would have stayed just another village in pretty anonymity, but writers such as Blunden and Charles Douie wrote vividly of its charms even when a war zone.

My love of the village and its inhabitants was born in 1997 when we bought a caravan on the bucolic site of Camping Bellevue or Camping Authuille, paraphrased brilliantly by our friend Bill George and known thereafter as Oatwheel.

The following are observations, through a series of sketches, of life at Oatwheel, the people, mainly French and British who really are, warts and all, human beings who are amusing, comical, whimsical, lugubrious, joyous, inspiring lovable, the list is endless.

If I have offended anyone, I apologise, although I suspect they deserve it.

Behind the inexhaustible woodpile below our window lives a fat man in shorts. I like him, he gardens with elan. Watching his annual progress to harvest is to watch a tidy man, even his netting hangs with Teutonic precision. To our right, overlooked by the tower of Thiepval, is another connoisseur of horticulture, always replete in flat cap and blue overall, he tends his plot, feeds his ducks and chickens religiously followed by his trusty hound. It has recently been very hot, so one day his cap failed to appear, the following his overall – a dire mistake, it rained.

Death begins this meandering. In early May while the weather excelled itself and rain was a figment of Somme mythology, a man who would not be tamed, who was larger than Brussels decided he had had enough and left us. An empty house to evoke memories of a multi-channelled TV which had no off-button, marauding, insatiable cats and unrivalled kindness and generosity; all that remain now are a declining garden, a reinvigorated bird population and a mural above the garage in tribute to poilu and Tommy who went before him 90 years ago. His widow, earth-mother, ethereal has returned to her Walloon roots to grieve, to try and assuage the loss of a gargantuan character who adored her.

Camping Bellevue has had its share of death from front-line Somme 1916 to the natural passing of an elderly population. Poona-like the British contingent intrigue, gossip and brag about their knowledge of the minor 'piece of bovver' that occurred round here. Most reside in the aptly named Spite Alley, a den of petty back-biting jealousy and slander. Thus, much like any street at home, the world spins on, from the desire to dig up a relative's grave because he was buried with his VC to accusations of overt-gonad scratching in female company, all is lost on the puzzled local who grins, gesticulates and exercises his patois to no avail on his audience.

Reginald Dixon's Francophile brother lives here too with his angelic wife. An organist and singer of some repute, sadly he is going blind; it does not affect his singing and playing or his driving round the site, but one is more worrying to his adoring audience than the other. Like so many of his age, National Service meant a civil war in Algeria, a time of innocence lost along with many comrades in circumstances that evoke tears even now.

Around the petanque area is the sojourn for passing travellers, marvelling at the pitch size and the rustic facilities. It is also possible to see the site's fattest man and the site's most petite woman; amazingly they are man and wife

Take the smallest caravan possible (imagine an anorexic shoe-box) hidden behind a deceptively big awning and there lived a family of four, shoe-horned into it – until recently when there are now only three. Unsettled by the available space made by the passing of Madam (no longer the delight of seeing her, sans-teeth, clad in floral dressing-gown carrying the overnight contents of a large bladder in a bucket) they have moved to a bigger home within pissing distance of the facilities.

Deep-Throat and his wife occupy a high position overlooking the central arena; this is their third move to our knowledge within the site. Whether this is because of their unpopularity (whispered allegations of moggy-murder) or a self-contained travel lust is impossible to say, but the fact remains that our friend's dog, Tommy, an inoffensive mutt of little intelligence and dubious parentage, without cause or warning, bit Deep-Throat (so-called because of his Jack Hawkins' impersonation). It was a moment of diplomatic crisis, not to mention the health and safety risks involved but fortunately Tommy was given the all-clear by the vet and after therapy and convalescence the status quo was resumed. Sensibly Deep Throat now goes to the facilities by a circuitous route across two fields, suitably chastened and wary of another incident which would inevitably result in his being 'put-down.'

Dogs are an integral part of Camping Bellevue and are stringently vetted before being allowed on. They must be a) small, b) have a high-pitched, grating yap and c) have the ability to utilize said yap at every conceivable opportunity day or night for whatever reason, and better still no reason at all. If they have the added bonus (a technical canine term!) of depositing personalised faeces prolifically they are assured of a hearty welcome, preferably in my opinion a double-barrelled one!

Cats are occasionally evident, most four-limbed and lethal, but next to us resides our three-legged feline friend who, whilst never letting us down, shows little interest in our presence. Which leads me to the elephant. Nellie, an elderly lady with the neatest of homes who seems to be regularly having to pack her trunk and depart for a few days to ascertain all is well with said Jumbo before returning afresh and hoovering her lawn. It is a revelation to us how often this happens but never forgetting anything must be most stressful.

At the end of the site is its Belgravia, its Mayfair, the poshest, most select and cultured part of the site and funnily enough we live there. Before our arrival it was a den of vice and drunken iniquity. Our neighbours, a fisherman and his surly wife, bulldog-like complete with salivating mouth, had two sons, the elder with domicile nearby and a face like thunder (in fact a very amicable chap) but with a problem with the 'sauce'. One sunny Sunday, returning from an over-indulgent session, he fell, or was he pushed, into a passing play pool. His popularity, already none too healthy, plummeted. Not content with this, another venture into alcohol led to raiding the fridge in the Chapiteau and a drunken foray through, yes through, an unsuspecting couple's tent in the early hours causing shock and possibly unwelcome coitus interruptus. Enough was enough and the supreme court of Desailly donned black cap and judged that he was never to darken Oatwheel's doorstep again. Now family pride intervened and his parents, our neighbours, fisherman and bulldog downed rods and left salivating profusely, in a huff and high dudgeon forever.

Another couple, the Whalleys, also left a mark (pronounced 'Whale-leys they were in fact Wallies); a couple on a mission to conquer the world of war cemeteries by having the ultimate photographic collection, they seduced the ever-willing Baz into helping them. Suddenly to the ever-present cackle of hysterical laughter, they lost interest in photos, web-site and most hurtfully in Baz, who licked his honourable wounds and retreated into his world of innocence, wondering why his and Mrs Baz' kindness had kicked them in the teeth.

Nudity for a short while lit up the mews depending on one's batting side: the middle-aged spectre of a masculine un-ironed body framed late at night in the door glass, followed by the filly from Paris flaunting her pedigree topless on the lawn. The heady appearance of the St Tropez scene proved a false dawn; the poorly-preserved matron did not hail from Paris and topless meant without a hat! She went the way of all temptresses once she realised that the only objects of possible seduction were all extremely elderly and were taking Viagra to stiffen the legs on their Zimmer-frames.

Opposite, the Wallies were replaced by an Ulster couple; a charming pair followed everywhere by two pretty little dogs, however you can't help feeling that the man with a twinkle in his eye, a lilt in his voice, may also have a gelignite store beneath my shed.

This select population is made complete by the new occupant of the home once owned by Monsieur Claude Balls, (or is it Clawed?), he is a tram driver from Lille, so full of his own brilliance that the fact that he is a cocky little shit seems not to trouble him at all.

An elderly lady Mme. Maigret, married to a long-deceased member of the 'Vieux Guillaume, or Vieux Guill, as it is fondly known; and a family of parents, grand-mother and children who personify the French en-famille complete the scene.

At the opposite extreme from the delights of the upper echelons of campsite life close to the 'Facilities' can be found, most of the time during the year, a collector of garden gnomes, Mr Slice. Unsurprisingly he resembles his petits-amis; short, squat, with a belly of elephant-like pregnancy. A sight much-dreaded if the weather turns hot, he is rumoured to have an eclectic collection of pornography, but whether its perusal affects him is difficult to judge as 50% of his body is an in the shade, out-of-sight mystery to all, not least himself.

The 'Facilities' are somewhat of a mis-nomer, in that they make nothing easier. A word of warning, never trust a cubicle lock, last year a naive young boy was trapped for so long he attempted to break the window and escape, in the process cutting his wrists, and it is rumoured that two elderly and portly matrons have not been seen since entering stoop toilet in the Ladies three years ago. Fortunately the latest Michelin-camping guide entry for "Oatwheel" also includes the phone numbers of the local Sapeur Pompiers and the Samaritans and urges visitors to learn them by heart.

It is time to turn to the most important, popular bi-lingual couple on the site with the most comprehensive social circle, the Amundsens – if you don't believe me, ask them! Hailing from the far-North they exhibit a touching mix of agnostic and disciple, cynic and hypocrite, admirable qualities that seem to endear them particularly to the French and in at least on the distaff side will ensure an easy and deserved entrance to Paradise. In addition to these myriad attributes their knowledge of the Great War is unsurpassed and they have visited everywhere of relevance, read every seminal text and know everyone of note. But most remarkable of all is her relationship with her 'boys,' heroes all, with not a fault or weakness amongst them.

It is most difficult to write objectively about these wonderful pilgrims and their selfless search of Remembrance and my eyes fill up thinking of their gallant lads in swirling kilts, sporrans and football scarves overwhelming the cowardly Hun to the strain of bagpipes and Jimmy Shand and I humbly crave for the understanding and empathy of the Amundsens, Christian soldiers forever onward.

Enough of the great and the good, let us turn to the bad – surprisingly a Welshman. Major X graced our campsite by not paying the rent on the smallest caravan ever seen and by being the most bigoted bastard that ever drew breath, even by the standards of the Principality. It is also unfair of me to point out that the rank of Major was that of an amateur, Territorial nature and the only action he ever saw was when trying to open a new bottle of rum after having already consumed one. One bad apple can affect the whole barrel, but this Granny Smith failed to do quitting the site for orchards new!

A new season beckons, not that you would know it from the "Camping Bellevue" web-site operating in a time warp. Two days into the 2011 season it resolutely shows 2010 information, but does it really matter, the place is unchanging, unaffected by climate change, fashion and strife.

The early residents come, tongues a-hanging in anticipation as soon as JC issues the first trickle of water through the dormant pipes. As for JC's winter chores, has he laid pathways for the cars on muddy days; has he trimmed the trees; fitted heating in the washrooms, done any of the multifarious tasks needed to improve the status of the site – no, but he has fitted new taps!

The inevitable progress of returning residents is always of interest, not least in those who have left this mortal coil since last year and do not appear. The effects of financial hardship; children growing up and being 'bored' with camping, these and many other reasons, real or imagined, wreak their toll on the population. It is also too early, and too cold to seduce the overnight traveller to rest his weary head on JC's homestead.

As for the overseas invader, our scouting mission and report on the state of play has little effect on those in the rear, in dribs and drabs they will appear, test their efficiency of closing down or not, and with consummate ease will slip into the comfortable apparel of rural French life. This year's pole position belongs to Pat and Barrie, newcomers to Oatwheel, very pleasant people, well-preserved, ex-military, who keep fit, drink moderately and keep to themselves, just the sort of qualities we try to avoid! But, worry not, on their tails are the reprobates who eschew everything not so healthy whom we love – the Huxtables, the Arshadis, followed by the Amundsens and the Bazzes.

Carol managed to break a tooth early on Thursday and in the heat of the moment a 200 mile round trip to the dentist loomed frighteningly, then in a moment of clarity it was remembered this is France, a civilized country, and they probably have dentists, so post haste to the big man at the Auberge and one phone call later an appointment the same afternoon in Albert.

So at 3 pm a slightly tentative Carol was dropped off, (with strict instructions to get out quickly if the dentist looked like Laurence Olivier – it's a movie joke and if you don't get it, tough) and by 3.30 emerged as good as new having forked out 40 euros - a bargain.

....

One time, on our return to the campsite, a new mobile-home had arrived. Ready for installation it lay tipped on its end like some ark-like leviathan ready to take in two by two those without sin on the campsite! How this monster mobile would be safely installed in its designated plot turned out to be the best free entertainment ever. Watched by a small, but enthusiastic audience: two men, a Land Rover, winch and ramps, the chosen equipment and with much pushing, pulling, turning and metaphorical greasing of the sides, the monster was tamed and today sits proudly in a double-plot, a veritable Colossus of the Campsite world.

....

We came back out here ten days ago and since then the weather has been constantly dire. It has lashed down with rain, battered our frail bodies with gale force winds and been cold enough to encourage a polar bear to invest in bed socks! Indeed, it has been so wet that the approach to our plot resembles Passchendaele in its muddiness.

Naturally this inclemency can be very depressing, and a healing libation the only answer in regular tinctures of a rather comfy little Bordeaux I know, and further remedial assistance at the local Auberge where our frequent attendance maintains standards; one must keep the natives on their toes, you know.

....

Wednesday was ANZAC Day, a celebration of the birth of two independent nations Australia and New Zealand, from the disaster that was Gallipoli. Various commemorations were held and countless Antipodeans made the long pilgrimage from Earls Court under trying circumstances, even though it involved having to imbibe the urine the French laughingly call beer and attempt to speak their impossible language. It is a source of wonder to the local inhabitants at the sheer number of hats with corks to be seen at this time of year, under which come forth stentorian cries of 'Bruce,' 'Sheila,' and 'Where's the f....king tinnies?'

The Digger connection was further enhanced by some friends of Barrie and Patricia's whom we met, one inevitably called Bruce, and his beautiful, sophisticated wife, who are as far removed from the Barrie Humphries caricature of 'a dinkum Aussie,' as I am from George Clooney, or even Rosemary for that matter! Erudite, well-read, cricket-loving and true battlefield pilgrims they were further evidence that our perceived superiority and arrogance over 'Colonials,' is totally erroneous. (I hasten to reassure my friends who know me well that this praise of all things Australian does not mean I am unwell, and there is little likelihood of a similar epiphany towards the Welsh, or me publicly admitting my paternal Grandma came from W....., there I nearly said it)

....

Here in the brave new world of a socialist France it is 9 pm
and hot, boy has it been hot for a few short days, in the upper
30s. However, we must not moan because the weather had
been shite and we can't have it both ways, although I'm sure
the odd clergyman and choirboy will disagree!

As I write, an hysterical duck in the field behind opens his
new book of 'One Hundred Jokes for Insomniac Ducks' and
begins to regale his large, captive audience whose ecstatic
appreciation lasts all night. The weather has dictated that the
harvest is late and must be undertaken when a dry moment
appears, at which time, usually during the hours of darkness, a
phalanx of wheezing combine harvesters practise hill starts
outside the bedroom window – Summer on the Somme.

My pathetic attempt at irony disguises the fact that we're
enjoying it here as always. Since we returned from finalising
Dad's ashes, we have been living la vie Francaise, this entails
driving very fast especially in supermarket car parks, kissing
everyone however ugly, imbibing copious amounts of vino
collapso and in our case visiting dead people, which has much
to recommend it.

The campsite is unusually quiet, whether it is the incessant
precipitation, or death that has kept the faithful from sniffing
their camping gaz is hard to assess. Also there are seven
mobile-homes for sale, an unheard of number and the site-
owner, one Jean-Claude, a lovely man, has taken the unheard
of step of 're-furbishing the facilities.' Rather than ripping
them down and re-building them, which is what they need,
this amounts to the proverbial lick of paint and nowt else!
This 'make-over' however is of great interest to those who are
staying here, watching the daily transfer of snot-green paint
from pot to walls via Jean-Claude's person, memorable, not
least as the walls come a poor second in their coverage.

No matter the site looks lovely and such perennial events as
the camp dinners have taken place. We have been present at
both orgies of Bacchanalia – the first dinner commenced at
mid-day and ground to a grisly end at 7.30 during which time

we worked our way through cocktails, vodka sorbet, white and red wine, a glass of champagne and a very generous digestif, not to mention a starter, main course of guineafowl, cheese and dessert, all for 20 euros! As you can imagine on a steaming hot day it took some stamina, but British fortitude and pluck (I think that's the word) carried the day.

As if this was a dress rehearsal, the following Saturday began with the camp photo, a motley crew as you can imagine, taken in the boules pitch and available on line from the Picardie Courier website under the heading 'Horrific Sight at Authuille.' From whence the eager campers ever enthusiastic at the prospect of a 'freebie' made their way to the Salle des Fetes for a couscous meal with copious booze and entertainment. I use this term 'entertainment' loosely. It was billed as, Franckie – Fakir l'Impossible!! and consisted of a seedy, elderly man in an ill-fitting wig dressed as a fakir accompanied by his equally elderly female assistant dressed in a belly-dancer's bikini performing magic. Well, it started as magic, eating razor blades, crushed light bulbs, assistant put in trunk and swords passed through etc but then became mutilation as he stuck long wire skewers through his arm, a tricky one this as his assistant had to use pliers to pull them through, his breast and finally his tongue. To finish members of the audience were asked up to pull them out! Fortunately, the couscous was glutinous enough to stay down!

A surreal, bizarre, revolting experience, enjoyed by some, but not by me, reminiscent of the seedy days of Victorian music-hall as portrayed in John Osborne's 'The Entertainer.' One is left feeling this could not have taken place in today's PC obsessed England, but here even the children were allowed to watch, most hiding behind their chairs fermenting tonight's nightmares in innocent minds.

The mobile-home garden burgeons, the runner beans are plentiful, the tomatoes a mouldy disaster, but no matter, the birds still sing, the vines ripen, the ghosts of citizen soldiers rest content in the golden fields and, in the sun-dappled woods, Authuille slumbers in the late summer sun, unchanged and unchanging.

....

Fat-Boy Slim moved house today, no literally, he moved his house from beside the Facilities (affectionately known as the Fatalities), that notorious perfumed oasis of cleanliness, to a vacant plot near us. It took over four hours; the help of the local farmer, his son and two tractors, as well as a motley crew of pushers, pullers, watchers and children of both sexes and indeterminate vintage.

Why did he move his home? Because he had indulged in a very public, very loud. slanging match with his neighbour in the boules pit watched by an appreciative audience of campers. Over what who knows? However, it was dire enough to lead to this extreme measure, up, off, wife and home together.

The afore-mentioned neighbour, a woman with children, it has to be said is a disappointment. Viewed from behind, long blonde hair, fine figure, enough to stir the elderly male campers' dormant memories, but when she turns round, age has indeed withered her and one's chagrin can only be compared to that of opening one's last and only bottle of an attentive little claret only to find that it is corked.

I digress, so Fat-Boy Slim decided to move home. They are not called mobile-homes for nothing – actually they are – there is nothing in the least bit mobile about them at all, especially when trying to manoeuvre the seven-ton receptacle of one's holiday dreams into a space an anorexic Mini would find testing.

The process of finally positioning the home was a highly technical process worthy of the nation who gave us Eiffel, Le Corbusier and Jean Nouvel and involved sitting on the tow-bar to raise the other end off the ground - the skill involved finding the correct weight. Now you may think Fat-Boy Slim the obvious answer but as I will explain later, not so. It was left to the bounteous figure of Raymond to supply the poundage necessary. All went well until the complaining tow-bar snapped, and another group discussion volubly ensued.

There were other casualties, too, Natalie's Mum's gate and hedge, not to mention the fence and hedge at the front of the plot, all without protest succumbed to the inexorable leviathan.

With much differing advice, many an 'ooh-la-la,' surprisingly little blasphemy, the placement of the home in the plot was finally achieved, the joint effort of a cosmopolitan assembly of a Chinaman, two Irish, two English and numerous Frenchmen – who says the UN is dead!

However, in the plot it might be but, it was so close, although parallel, to the alley that the decking would be IN the alley, so it was decided to push it sideways down the worrying slight slope with the tractor on thin boards placed under the wheels. It was suggested (by a non-Frenchman, I must add) the boards be greased with olive oil, virgin, of course, to ease its progress – this heresy was immediately shouted down.

Eventually, tortuously, one badly-scratched mobile home was moved enough to suffice; vast barrels of T-Cut were ordered; large sods replaced in the grass beneath; a celebratory bottle opened and some sort of normality returned to Oatwheel.

What the neighbour left behind will think when she turns up, only to find her bête noir has been spirited away into appropriately thin air, remains to be seen. No doubt she will hurriedly re-check the amount of ingredients recommended, in her well-thumbed tome, 'Livre Femme de la Magie, Chapitre 5, 'Voisins – au revoir.'

Oh yes, you might be wondering, why Fat-Boy Slim? Until last year he was larger than a skip full of Eric Pickles (my apologies if you're eating your tea) but over one winter he has transformed himself into Monsieur le Svelte! An achievement not to be taken lightly, especially when you see the look of delight, nay relief on the face of his diminutive wife.

....

In the words (almost) of the immortal Ronnie Barker, 'It's been a funny old year.' Today as we pack to leave, letting Jean-Claude and other natural, but also often unseen, residents of the campsite, iron their pyjamas, check essential supplies of claret, fromage and much more, draw a deep, elderly comfortable chair in front of the fire and with a specially selected edition of 'Le Figaro' (face-shading dimensions), set the alarm for March.

For the temporary resident it has been a time of death and sadness; of illness and mutilation; of friends made and friends moving on, and dreadful weather. The most appropriately named Angele, finally, tired out, lost her battle to cancer; a lady who exuded love, warmth and friendship but whose passing meant her equally wonderful husband, Maurice, 'Mo-Mo', Oatwheel's Maurice Chevalier, had to leave too as he had lost his sight and could not drive – their caravan still for sale, scene of so many happy times, a poignant memorial to them both.

Another younger resident, Alain, lost his fight, too – the insidious Gauloise added another notch to its packet. I did not like him much, once describing him as a 'cocky little shit,' nothing changed, but I salute his guts.

Sadly, a number of residents have packed up their bags and have moved out, this is due to illness, old age, straitened financial circumstance or like John Marie and Francoise they have decided on a change of scenery: after fifteen years, one battlefield for another, the Great War for the D Day beaches, the Somme for Utah Beach.

I end this with the weather – it's raining, but from our window Aveluy Wood is slowly putting on her autumn hues, the birds are singing, our web-footed comedian friend is regaling his enthralled audience with the latest edition of risqué duck humour and the air is redolent with the comforting smell of freshly-ironed pyjamas and a semblance of distant snoring.

It's hard to leave but a nasty little virus drives us home early, but Oatwheel will be in our thoughts till we come through those gates eager, expectant next March (if J-C remembers to open them!) re-invigorated and ready for 'owt!

Bon Nuit J-C

....

It's nine o'clock at night after a scorching day; across the valley Aveluy Wood is bathed in soft, hazy sunlight as the sun reluctantly fades behind the skyline. A desultory train meanders along the valley; the church clock lazily chimes the hour, a cooling breeze rustles the restless trees. Along the alley comes the smell of a well-done barbeque, the sound of the important business of opening – tin, bottle, essential supplies and Gallic conversation, gentle, persuasive and pleasant to the ear.

Across the lane to Lonsdale Cemetery the ever-present ducks regale each other with another joke; the family hound listens ears cocked from the window in the shed where it sleeps, but, mutt that he is fails, to appreciate the subtleties of canard humour and flops down dreaming of being let loose in the duck pen.

The road up the hill next to the wood leads to Mesnil but also to what the Tommy called Brock's Benefit, after the well-known firework manufacturer. To get to it from here you must walk past the church to the war memorial; a fairly standard issue, the head and shoulders of an armless poilu on a plinth with a dozen names or so who left this little village and died for Mother France. A Desailly is there, lost amongst the many; I wonder if he had the family face, peasant, but warm, open, trustworthy?

The flowers here and all over the village are maintained by the mayor, a stolid, square citizen who has the perpetual Gaulois cemented to his bottom lip, usually to be seen in shorts perfecting the lines of potatoes behind our home. Phlegmatic, unfazed, a man of the soil, I like him.

Down the hill we go and come to the Ancre, beloved by Blunden, a friendly, happy little river, but not before passing our beloved Auberge, silent tonight, it's Monday, but the lure of Bourgogne magic still lingers here.

To the left a small house, now a gite, but once the home of a big man in every sense, now gone to be larger than life in Walloon Valhalla, never to be forgotten.

The sun has gone now and I go no further tonight, where better to end this flight of fancy, beside the Ancre, between the abode of two dear friends, one stilled forever, but eternally in our thoughts; the other also larger than life, a terrible man, serial killer and chef extraordinaire. A perfect pair of bookends!

....

A SCOTSMAN'S LETTERS FROM GALLIPOLI AND EGYPT 1915-16

"Let those who come after see to it that his name be not forgotten"

The photos, mementoes and a number of sun bleached letters tell the story of Archie Alexander, Corporal in the I/5th Battalion, The Royal Scots Fusiliers. He looks out steadily from his photograph - fresh-faced, innocent, handsome but proudly a soldier. A soldier from Ayr Road, Irvine in the county of Ayr, one of three brothers [Hugh and Jamie survived the War] and a sister. Archie was employed before the conflict by the Glasgow & South-western Railway. Today at St Enoch's Station you will see his name, alongside 301 other employees who gave their lives for King and Country, on a memorial unveiled in 1922 by Earl Haigh.

The story begins with the mementoes of a soldier - the brass cigarette box given at Christmas 1914 redolent with patriotism and military glory. "Imperium Britannicum" it proudly proclaims and is surrounded by names martial - Servia, Montenegro, Russia, Japan, France, Belgium. A tattered envelope holds three pristine ribbons of the 1914 Star, the British War Medal and Victory Medal. "Pip, Squeak and Wilfred"; sadly someone stole the actual medals; a soldier's New Testament dated Stirling 1914 inscribed "Love Life" and most poignantly a faded identity disc, faint but discernible "7611 A.Alexander 5RSF."

Archie Alexander was to be found in 1914 in the 1/5 Battalion TF South Scottish Brigade, Lowland Division, in May 1915 becoming 155th Brigade, 52nd Division. It is evident that he was a prolific and natural letter writer in an elegant, educated hand. The first surviving letter is from Cambusharron, estimated date 14 May 1915 just before he left for the Mediterranean.

"Everything up here is a splitter and I have been working in the Orderly Room all week and will likely be there until we move off. No one seems to know when but from what we are told it will likely be about Tuesday or Wed. Our destination I hear is Egypt then from there work our way up the Dardanelles so at last I will be able to see a bit of life and trust in good luck to get thro' safely — The voyage I understand is about 10 to 12 days so this will make up for the cruises I won't get this year! — I was up before the Officer today and I am to get another stripe and I may get it before we go off, so I think I am not badly off either, and it is always a little to show I have been keeping clear of any trouble and I'll be doing my best at all times."

Archie, in fact sailed from Liverpool on the Mauretania on Friday 21 May and reached Mudros on the 29th and Gallipoli, Cape Helles sector, on 6 June. The regimental history states that even on the day of the landing the Brigade "were heavily shelled in the first rest camp". It is apparent that at some time between then and early July Archie was wounded in the stomach. In a letter to his sister, unfortunately the first page is missing but it is post marked 11 July, he states that "he sent a letter to Mum from here" [Malta] on 11 July and signs it "Baldic."

"Malta is a fine island and a very nice and convenient place to bring the wounded. [He reports the local paper giving the temperature as 132F]. — It is something similar on the Peninsula where we are engaged and it don't make matters any more comfortable for us. — I heard our Brigade was being re-enforced by some Highland regiments. I have had the experience of seeing our naval forces in action up here and they can't half make the Turks know they are here."

Aug 23rd Fort Ricolozi [Malta]

"at above place convalescent. I will be here no more than a week, then I go to Alexandria in Egypt — from there back to the Dardanelles to rejoin my regiment — I have four mates here some Australians and they are fine fellows."

From Malta Archie moved to Alexandria from where he wrote on 1 September, having arrived the day before, on notepaper headed "Church Army Recreation Tent, Mediterranean Expeditionary Force."

"I am now at Mustafa Barracks, Alexandria, Egypt arriving here yesterday after a 3 day sail from Malta. This is the final clearing station where you get equipped and passed fit again for the Dardanelles. — I just about failed to pass the Doctor yesterday. You know he saw my old wounds and was quite surprised. He asked me all about them and brought me up again and said I would have to get an abdominal belt. — I will go back on the first draft from here, probably in a week or less. — It is another 3 day sail from here to the D. so I fancy

I will soon be a sailor let alone a soldier. Is Johnnie Tulloch's regiment out yet I think their lot are for France. — The Sgt I mated with in the trenches and was taking care of my letters when I was away was wounded in the charge of July 12th, so no saying when I'll see him again."

The un-named Sergeant was probably wounded in the attack on 12 July between Kereves Dere and Achi Baba nullah. The division lost over 4,800 killed or wounded, "In large areas between Tweed and Forth scarcely a household but mourned a son" so wrote John Buchan [History of the Royal Scots Fusiliers].

It seems likely that Archie left Egypt around 8 September and returned via Lemnos to Gallipoli. His first letter written from the Peninsula is dated 29 October and most of his weekly epistles have survived. It is interesting in reading John Buchan's description of this time on the Peninsula he might almost be echoing Archie.

"The troops had to sit still in their stifling trenches and every acre of that butt-end of Gallipoli was searched by the enemy's fire. Under such conditions - inaction, grave losses, grave discomforts - it was a marvel that men maintained so high a spirit and so steady a cheerfulness."

October 29th 1915

"I am in the firing line and having my short spell off so I am pleased to use my time this way. No doubt things out here will be appearing as quiet to folks at home, quite true in a sense but busy enough for those actually concerned. The Turk and his German advisors try to harass us as much as possible keeping us very much on the alert and taking no chance. Trench warfare is — ? We have a lot of mining, sapping and getting at him with Bombs and many an anxious time he has.

I have just got over a short spell in a hot corner of a bombing sap after doing our best to oust some of their snipers from an awkward position. — You would not know me I have not shaved my lip for over 2 months and have a fancy moustache, eh? — We lost another of our old officers the other night — Chris Vivers a fine fellow he was too. Shot thro' the throat by a sniper in this part we are in now. He was a schoolmaster in Ayr Ac."

November 4th

"After I left Egypt I was sent to a place called Lemnos a Greek island not far from here I wrote you to say — was well but the letters were under a strict censor -- I am still in the firing line and making the best of it. There is not a great deal of heavy fighting this time but we are having it hot enough at times. It has been a big success we have had in France but I see it has cost a great many lives. I was sorry to see of George Donaldson being killed. He was unfortunate poor fellow and he is very young too. It's a great war, but it must come to an end sometime or other. — It is dark now by 6 o'clock which means extra work for us as we have to mount guard whenever darkness sets in and keep a look out in case of attack."

17th November

"We came up into the firing line on Sunday and have kept at it since then I can tell you. 1 can't say much but I'll risk a little. We attacked the Turks on Monday 15th and gained our objective then they made a counter attack on us during the following night but they were repulsed after some hard fighting as we knew they would try to recover lost ground we were fully prepared. It was quite an anxious time and to make matters worse it poured almost all night and thunder and lightning was awful but I came thro' it all right. — We also blew up a mine underneath their trench. Talk about an explosion it could be heard above the heavy shelling and rifle fire. — You will see I am still a Lance Cpl yet. Well I don't fancy my chance of ever being any more. I missed my chance of promotion while away in hos. and now there are almost as many N.C.O.'s as men in the Coy but I don't worry as I am as content one way as another."

25th November

"Mrs Tulloch will be in a bad state about Johnnie [Lance Cpl John Tulloch, 7th Cameron Highlanders killed at Loos 25 Sept 1915] and I also see where Alex [?] has been wounded, bad enough too. He will be the lucky man who comes thro' all this without a scratch. I have a lot to be thankful for —? and there's nothing like taking things as they come and making the best of everything."

On 7 December the positions at Anzac and Suvla were evacuated. The task of the 155th Brigade was to "distract the enemy." This was mainly in the line in small bombing enterprises around Krithia nullah.

8th December

"I am in the firing line again. My mate on the sentry post beside me got wounded first night up the bullet going in at one shoulder and out the other. He was one of my old platoon and there are very few of us left by now I was just counting. Out of 48 men who came out with us only 1 Sgt, 2 Cpls, 4 Lan Cpls and 11 men are left. The rest are either killed or wounded or away sick. It is 6 months past on Monday since we first landed here [6 June] and the battn. has never had a rest away from here during that time. I was lucky getting my spell off. But it will come to a finish sometime sooner or later. I see Johnny Tulloch has been reported killed. It is hard lines I was reading a column about him in the Troon and Prestwick Times."

In his next letter, a very hurried, brief affair with evidence of the censor's blue pencil, Archie was obviously involved in the evacuation of Gallipoli.

Jan 4th 1916

"This is all I can tell you but hope to have good news for you soon."

By now the 155th Brigade had been relieved on 31 December and evacuation took place on the 7 - 8 January, the last troops being off by 03.30 on the 9th. Archie went with the 1/5th Battalion to Egypt and the next letter continues the story.

Feb 29th 1916

"I am in the desert, no sign of life except Arabs with their camels. Very little water and what is has to be boiled before we can use it. But dear Mother, I am content and thankful to be here."

March 5th, Cairo

"I am now away from the desert again. I came here yesterday to undergo a 3 week course of Instruction for Non-Commissioned Officers. So many from each Battalion are represented, two of us are here and glad I am to get back to civilisation again. - Where we were doing duties before I came here was 8 miles right into the desert and you hardly realise what it is like. Nothing but sand. We were doing outpost duty always night work but it's the game. You did not get washed twice a day there. All the water that we got was brought to us in tanks carried by camels and we used it all for cooking. But I am seeing both sides of life now and it will do me no harm. - I remember often he [Archie's father] told me when I first listed that the war would last longer than we thought. - Inside you get a snapshot Jamie Couper took of me. It's no good I am twisted into an awful shape but I'll send you it, but don't let anyone see it."

March 29th

"Talk about heat-you feel like being roasted out here."

April 7th

"I have been issued with light khaki. That is light togs for the heat. Shorts above the knees nice and cool and of course the sun helmet which we have had for some time. We do duty here in short sleeves and it's hot as you may guess. I am in the desert again miles from nowhere doing rather important duties, getting it hard enough too but still smiling. You were asking if my visit to Cairo was a forerunner to promotion. Well in a sense I fancy my chance in fact I'm first for anything that's going but no saying when that may be. I and a few others of the "old firm" consider we have been been done dirty as regards promotion. You see we have been getting drafts of reinforcements sent out from home lately to make up our losses we had on Gallipoli. Well with these drafts come out lots of Sgts, Cpls etc who have seen no fighting at all and they are put in the same footing as we are, but I'm not worrying any. I've done not too bad and am content. Hugh I hope is keeping at it. Tell him from me mind No 1 always. I'm not what is called an old soldier but I know a thing or two now."

The last letter is dated 15 April 1916. It confirms the impression of a fine young man determined to make the best of it, determined to keep smiling and do his duty, however onerous with efficiency and pride.

"I have now shifted another 9 miles further into the desert and instead of writing "somewhere" I use nowhere for this is No

Man's Land right enough. My company is doing very important Outpost duties. Nothing but the desert sands for company except for the daily visit by the camels with our water and rations but through it all I keep smiling. It will come to an end sometime. Tell him [his brother Jamie who has also enlisted] to keep his heart up, put all his heart and soul into it, don't trust too much to anyone and mind No 1 he won't go wrong. — This Derby 2 affair will be making some of the slackers hop. I only wish I had some of them out here having a taste of this. They may be sorry they did not take their chance along with the others. Soldiering is bad enough without having to do it against your will eh. but I suppose they will get the same thanks as the rest of us once it's over, but that don't worry me in the least."

The final chapter in Archie's tragic but familiar story takes place on 23 April 1916, Easter Sunday. He was shot in the head at an outpost El Ducidar and died instantly. However, there is an intriguing confusion about the circumstances of his death. Amongst his letters is a detailed diagram sent to a "Mr Dickie Irvine per R.Couper which has these annotations on it.

"1/5th RSF 'A' Company at El Dueidar
Easter Sunday 1916
Outpost El Dueidar
Strength 120 1 Platoon fully equipped and ready [A.A.]
Attacked 5.10 a.m.

Cpl AA & 3 or 4 men went out to reinforce No 1 Post [3 men & NCO] & found the post garrison driven out & at about X AA led men back to their post & was fatally wounded in head in doing so. Stopping the original Garrison from retiring he took initiative."

Most mysterious of all is the cryptic message at the bottom of the page "I could say very much more."

Also included is a letter to Archie's parents dated 6 June from P. Ritchie.

"Although we were not in the same Battn I knew that he would be always ready & willing to make any sacrifice asked of him — While he was in charge of a small outpost I learned from his men that he was trying to locate a sniper who had been troubling him, but unfortunately the sniper got his shot in first and so he died trying to save his comrades. Could anything be so brave that he should up his life for others. It might be a little consolation to know that he got a decent burial and his grave is marked with a beautiful cross. I seen him laid to his last long rest, and all the Dreghorn boys were there too. Archie is sorely missed in his own Battalion as he was one of the best and most esteemed N.C.O.'s and he is also missed by all the Dreghorn men."

There is an obvious discrepancy between these two accounts of Archie's death. It is equally obvious that Ritchie would want to avoid any controversy in a letter to Archie's parents but the speculation must be from the notes on the diagram, the last sentence that the men from No 1 Post were driven out in disarray, were perhaps even running away, and that Archie rallied them and persuaded them to do their duty as he thought opportune and honourable. In doing so he was killed. Whatever the truth both accounts are agreed on Archie's qualities as a soldier and as a man.

On 12 May the fateful Army Form 13104-82 was sent to Archie's parents at Cemetery Lodge, Irvine, with those devastating three words written immaculately in ink "Killed in Action." A faded photograph of Archie's original grave remains with 18 other names accompanying his, all killed that same day. Today Archie lies in Grave 220 Row F, Kantara War Memorial Cemetery on the eastern side of the Suez Canal, 50 kilometres south of Port Said.

His two brothers, Hugh and Jamie, survived the war but both died young as the result of wounds received: Jamie in 1924 and Hugh in 1930.

Let the final words come from Archie himself as he closed what was to be his last letter, full of the typical goodness and humanity which he displayed at all times.

"I'll now close as I'll have to get my rifle cleaned again and off for another 12 hours night duty. It's all night work here so ta ta meantime and trusting my dear Father and keep well and remember me to all my friends. Love to all. Your loving Son Archie xxxx"

Acknowledgement: The letters are reproduced by kind permission of Archie's descendants, the Lawley family of Harlow, Essex.

AN OLD CHUM OF MINE

At the top of the High Street in the picturesque little Essex market town of Saffron Walden proudly stands the war memorial inscribed with the names of 159 of her sons who did not return from the Great War. One of them has always struck a chord with me, not just because of the tragedy of his story, but also because of his courage and commitment. To me he has become a fondly remembered old chum whose grave I often visit when I am in France.

Tom Smith came from a large family who lived in one of the neat, orderly cottages to be found today just yards away from the war memorial on which his name resides. After attending school locally, Tom, finding employment difficult, followed thousands of his fellow-countrymen and emigrated to New Zealand where he became a farmer, working his own piece of land at Kumeur, Kaipara.

When war clouds loomed, Tom continued to work his farm until in 1918 when the sense of guilt that he was safe and far away from the dangers of the Western Front became too much for him. Tom decided his country needed him more than his farm, so he volunteered and was posted to C company 38th. New Zealand Expeditionary Force Reinforcements.

After initial training Tom embarked for the Mother Country on the H.M.N.Z.T. No. 105 "Rumuera" at Wellington. In England, he spent a further eight weeks with the New Zealand Rifle Brigade (N.Z.R.B) in further training at Brocton, before being shipped to France on September 25th.

Prior to his departure for the front, Tom came home to Saffron Walden one last time to say his farewells. This leave, however, was of special significance because whilst staying with his brother, he and his sister-in-law unavoidably fell in love; a potentially traumatic situation avoided by his leaving for France.

I was told this poignant tale in 2000 by Tom's niece, an elderly lady who related that her mother's secret love lasted the rest of her life, unknown to all but her daughter in whom she confided. At the time I was researching the war dead of Saffron Walden for my book, The Victor Heroes, but I had to promise that I would not use this information while she was still alive. Now she is no longer with us, I thought you might like to hear this tale, another broken heart of the Great War.

On September 25th for the journey to the station, his family hired a handsome coach and horses to transport their hero on the first stage of his journey to the Front, a distance of some 500 yards! What a sight it must have been!

Once in France, he was sent to Etaples, where, at the notorious "Bull-Ring", he was "toughened up" for the front-line. He joined 'C' company of his battalion on September 30th. in the vicinity of Cambrai, where the Allied push was in full swing.

On October 8th. 1918, he received multiple wounds and died in the 29th. Casualty Clearing Station where he had been taken.

Tom had been in France a mere twelve days, in the front-line only eight and he was thirteen days away from his fortieth birthday. He was never again to see the green and rolling hills of his lonely farm.

Tom's tragic story is by no means unique, but he symbolizes all that is honourable in the story of the Great War - his desire to 'do his bit' despite his age; his brief existence as a soldier and the woman who loved him and her daughter who understood and, despite having never met him, remembered him with great affection and immense pride.

"GOLDEN AND RARE"

One day in 1944 the contents of a room that had been locked in time for nearly thirty years, including numerous stuffed otter heads - trophies of hunting days-were taken outside Newport House and burnt - they were the treasured remains belonging to the only son of Alfred and Ellen Barthropp.

The room had been regularly and lovingly cleaned but remained exactly as it had been in January 1915 when the shattering news came of the death in France of the Barthropp's only son, Sidney. By 1944 his father had died and his mother Ellen had become too aged to maintain the big house and so was moving away to Sussex.

Sidney Barthropp was the first casualty of the Great War from Newport, a village very close to where I live in Saffron Walden. The effect on a close-knit village was immense, as the family had lived there since 1894 and had fully involved themselves in local affairs since their arrival. When the Boer War began in 1899 Sidney's father Alfred Barthropp had lent flags to decorate the Parish Hall for a concert to raise funds for soldiers' families.

Alfred had joined the Militia in May 1889 aged 37 and remained until retiring aged 55 in 1907. At some stage he volunteered for the Great War, despite being over 60, and remained in the Suffolk Regiment, before working at the depot of the Norfolk Regiment and conducting drafts to France at Boulogne. He probably left the army in April 1918. He and Ellen became proud parents of Sidney Alfred Nathaniel Shafto on 25th March 1892 (the name Shafto is familiar in the well-known Northumbrian ballad, 'Bonny Bobby Shafto' from whose family Alfred was descended on his mother's side).

Sidney was born in Kensington and went to Winchester public school, where in his last year he was a House Prefect and played in the Commoners XV. He went up to Trinity College, Cambridge in 1910, and taking his degree in 1913 went on to Bishop's Hostel at Farnham with the intention of studying for the Church. He was devoted to field sports and was a keen student of natural life: he would sometimes stay out all night observing the habits of badgers and foxes. His fondness for, and eager participation in, all sorts of country pursuits earned him amongst his fellow students the name of 'The Squire.' In June 1914 he was chosen to be Master of the Eastern Counties Otter Hounds.

However, it was short-lived as on August 4th war was declared and Sidney immediately joined the 3rd Bn. Royal Sussex Regt. (Special Reserve) then at Dover. On January 11th 1915 he joined D Company, 2nd Battalion in France, setting in motion a tragic story, mirroring that of countless other young men of similar backgrounds who became members of the most vulnerable ranks of soldier killed in the Great War, the Second-Lieutenants and Lieutenants. He was posted to the same sector of the Western Front as Robert Graves (author of 'Goodbye to All That').

Britain in 1914 had an army with less than a quarter of a million men available for immediate service in Europe. The basic unit of the foot soldier was the platoon of up to 50 men under the command of either a Lieutenant or a Second Lieutenant. The official title of these two junior officers was subalterns, however they were often called 'warts.'

Any man over the age of 18 and with a private school education was deemed officer material and given the minimum of training to make him competent to lead his men into battle at the outbreak of war. Many were still at school, at university or had just left, eager for adventure, worried the war might be over by Christmas and that they would miss it. For Sidney Barthropp, however, the great adventure lasted only a fortnight: he was killed in action in the trenches in the brickfields, near Cuinchy on 29th January 1915. He was 22 years of age.

The engagement in which he was killed became known as the Battle of the Keep. At 1900 hours on the 28th January 1915 the 2nd battalion of the Sussex Regiment relieved the 1st Loyal North Lancs in the Brickstacks trench line at Cuinchy in the La Bassée Canal (South) sector. B and A Companies held the trench running south from the canal and railway-line embankment (known as 'Trench 3') and D Coy, commanded by Captain Villiers, held the 'Keep' adjoining them. The 'Keep' was an apt name, for, in line with its medieval title, the Germans attacked it equipped as for an attack during a medieval siege, with scaling ladders and axes, along with bomb and bullet.

It was to the east of Cuinchy church and was a British-held strongpoint made from a reinforced series of brickstacks among the brickfields largely held by the Germans. After the German attacks on the 25th January, it was in a more exposed position and at 0800 hours on the 29th January, the Germans began a determined attack upon both the 'Keep' and the trenches immediately around it. One large and two small Minenwerfers bombarded it for 45 minutes and then German infantry attacked it on three sides. D Company, however, put up a stout resistance. Robert Graves wrote 'The Germans are very close; they have half the brickstacks, we have the other half. Each side snipes down from the top of its brickstacks into the other's trenches'.

Acting CSM Butcher skillfully controlled the Company bombing parties with their improvised bombs and, with the withering marksmanship of the riflemen, kept the German attackers from the 'Keep' walls. Even so, some parties of Germans got to within 10 yards of the 'Keep'. Shortly afterwards the 1st Northants, also of 2nd Brigade, put in an attack to the south-east of the 'Keep' and the Royal Artillery started to find its targets. By 12.30 hours the Germans had called off the attacks and had resorted to shelling the British positions. During the German attack, however, thirteen members of 2nd Sussex were killed, including Sidney Barthropp who was shot through the head by a sniper, and died instantly.

Col EWB Green, Second Lieutenant Barthropp's commanding officer, wrote to his parents:

"He was killed during an attack by the Germans upon a portion of the line which we were holding, and in which the company with which your son was serving put up a very gallant defence and beat off a very determined attack. He died a soldier's death in the very front of the fight. In him we feel we have lost a comrade who was bound to do well, and who during the short time he had been with us had endeared himself to all."

It was recorded by the adjutant that when he was shot he had been firing from the trench at the oncoming German soldiers, many of whom were yards away, and some had even invaded the trenches occupied by the British. The chaplain also wrote to Sidney's parents to let them know that there had been a proper burial in the graveyard, the Cuinchy Communal Cemetery near Bethune, and gave precise directions to the grave for future reference. During the burial lyddite shells could be heard, and he remarked on the bullets whizzing by those attending. Sidney was 22 years old and had been confirmed in his rank as 2nd Lieutenant the day he was killed.

When the telegram carrying the terrible news arrived, Major Barthropp was himself away on duty but he hurried back to be with his wife. Ellen Barthropp bore the loss of her only son bravely, unpacking herself his returned belongings, her stoicism only shaken by the unexplained loss of his watch!

Today Sidney's name heads the list of 41 Newport dead of the Great War on the war memorial and in the church to the right of the chancel arch (sadly partly hidden by the organ) is a family plaque. In addition, because his mother came from a military family, the Wentworth Stanleys of Longstowe, Cambridgeshire, there is, in the church of St Mary, a Wall tablet to Sidney with the Winchester College coat of arms on the left, the Barthropp's coat of arms in the centre and the family motto (Foy en tout – faith in all). The tablet incorrectly spells his place of death, Cuinchy, as Quincy.

The individual personal tragedy of Sidney Barthropp is reflected in the huge losses of so many of the young men who might have become leaders of their generation, and the fathers, guides, tutors and leaders of the next generation. As a modern writer concludes in his study of every aspect of a subaltern's life and death.

'They were golden and rare. They pleasantly sabotage stereotypes.'

CENTENARY OF THE BATTLE
OF THE SOMME 2016

It is 21.30 the night before the world changed – 100 years ago. Forgive me if I dare to profess that I am nervous, the morrow beckons and remembrance, sadness, pride and expectation are strange bedfellows. It is raining, cloudy, none too warm, very different from so long go, in the Past. But is it another country as L P Hartley described it? I think it is not in many ways; the weather may be, but memories link the years for much longer than generations. My beloved Grandad, who survived the battle of Arras, lived till he was 82, overlapping by 12 years my life; his memories and mine span 144 years.

Dusk falls, memories stir, it is nine and a half hours till we have to be at the airport; the same time as the Big Push began, as the mines erupted and until their whistles blew a hundred years ago...........

Inevitably we were nervous of something delaying our progress to the airport at Albert where we were to park the car and pick up our shuttle bus. Despite a slow-moving queue of cars which we joined a mile or so before the airport, we were parked, had been through security, given a bag of ephemera to entertain and educate us and were on our way to Thiepval, ironically passing our campsite entrance an hour after we had left it.

The site at Thiepval had been transformed, marquees, walkways, portaloos and we had plenty of time to take it all in as we joined a queue that snaked via the Visitors' Centre, which was packed with shoppers and browsers as well as those thrifty visitors trying to get into the newly-opened museum whilst entrance was free!

At the end of the queue was the opportunity to gain another bag if you'd missed it earlier and obtain the very impressive programme, in the language of your choice, French or English that is.

It is time I mentioned the weather, it was cool, breezy, grey-leaden skies and a definite hint of inclement weather to come. The approach to the monument on this side, the Ulster Tower side, consisted of, on the right, a marquee the length of the approach where coffee, croissants and cakes satisfied the inner man, to be accurate, more the inner woman. On the left a tank, a Sopwith Camel and various displays in small 'far-pavilion' style marquees.

We decided to return to the museum to see if we could get in; a silly idea as people were still queuing, but we did get into the shop where I indulged in a vanity trip to see how many of my poetry books were on the shelf and then plan to return at the end of the day and marvel, open-mouthed at how many had been sold to eager punters!

It was time to take our seats which, after a short wait, we did. I will not try to explain where these were in relation to the monument, albeit we had access to three big screens and we were happy with our lot.

I will refrain from a detailed résumé of the event, suffice to say that when we, the Brits, decide to put on something like this, there is no-one in the world who can compare, let alone better.

Reflections and memories include the massed lines of the Guards' Regiment in the bearskins and scarlet tunics, matched by those of the French band in their Franco-Prussian style uniforms; the choice of music, particularly that of George Butterworth, elegiac and haunting; the perfectly chosen readings – I have never heard Rosenberg's 'Break of Day in the Trenches,' read so well; the wonderful voices of Charles Dance and Joley Richardson, as narrators linking the readings, most of which were written by casualties of the Great War, casualties whose names are to be found amongst the 73,000 on the great memorial behind.

The entrance of the King's Troop Royal Horse Artillery, towing the 13 pounder quick fire guns which had actually seen service on the Somme, marked the end of the two-minutes' silence and the fall of poppies and cornflowers from the monument, a final act of Remembrance as children from France and the United Kingdom laid wreaths on each of the graves in the Anglo-French cemetery.

The weather toyed with us, it remained cloudy although the sun did make a brief appearance, as did a heavy shower leading to the unveiling of the free plastic poncho supplied by CWGC for such an occasion. I refrained from this preferring to get wet, which I did, rather than sitting there looking like a supermarket carrier-bag rack.

I was most impressed by the dignitaries; a close-up during the silence showed their faces intense, serious and clearly moved. Charles read Masefield beautifully, Kate looked stunningly elegant and the dear old Mayor of Authuille, Regis, or Bognor as I affectionately call him, looked thoroughly at home amidst such exalted company including President Hollande, although I'm sure he was gasping for a Gauloise!

The Service over, it was time for lunch provided free in a neat little brown paper carrier bag, comprising of a mixture of filled rolls, poncey ones like wholemeal, a chocolate brownie, a piece of quiche, a currant bun, mine, though still tasty, had been sat on, I think, an apple and an orange drink. I'm not sure what the French thought of it, but to us unsophisticated Anglo-Saxons, it wasn't bad.

We had to shelter from the rain under the trees to consume this feast, but it eased as we finished and we took the opportunity to climb up the steps to the memorial and lay our wreath to George Cornell, at the Essex Regiment panel 10D, one of four Saffron Walden 1st July deaths, The steps and war stone were awash with poppies, many wreaths with photos, many with poignant messages.

Down into the cemetery where the flowers and wreaths seemed even more vibrant after the recent shower before going for a final refreshment whilst waiting for a bus.

Bill met us briefly and then we tried to fulfil our earlier plan to return to the museum/bookshop, a well-planned move which foundered on the fact that most of the invited throng had the same idea.

So the bus was our most viable option, as it was, again, for everyone else, but ever-resourceful Rose played the Parkinson card and with the help of some brilliant young soldiers we were aboard a bus toute suite!

We were fading now, but once back at the airport, after a little difficulty in locating our car, we were soon on our way back via a most circuitous route in the opposite direction to what we needed, but once we remembered we had a 'laissez-passe' to allow us into the restricted zone we sailed regally through the road blocks and were home by 5.30 pm, tired but triumphant.

Final thoughts – it was a magnificent day we shall never forget. It was the greatest privilege to honour those who had died and the organisation of the ceremony was exemplary, one could not fault it in any way. The choice of music, readings, the quality of the readers; the discipline of the bands, the professionalism of it all was without parallel. The weather could have been better, but it became irrelevant we were at something very special.

I am left with a sense of pride, proud to be English, proud that no-one in the world could have equalled it, let alone bettered it. Delighted that every French friend who was there was so fulsome in their praise of it all that it made one's heart sing.

One of the names on Thiepval, is Hector Hugh Munro, better known by the pen name Saki, a writer of witty, mischievous, cynical and sometimes macabre stories. Over-age to enlist and refusing a commission he joined the 2nd King Edward's Horse as an ordinary trooper. He later transferred to the 22nd Battalion of the Royal Fusiliers, in which he rose to the rank of lance sergeant. More than once he returned to the battlefield when officially still too sick or injured. In November 1916 he was sheltering in a shell crater when he was killed by a German sniper, his last words were "Put that bloody cigarette out!' Cynic he may have been, but I believe even he would have approved.

4TH JULY 2016

SAYING GOODBYE TO DAD - TUESDAY 31st JULY 2012

What started as the relatively simple task of disposing of Dad's ashes became a black comedy of Orton-esque proportion.

We felt it was right to add his ashes to those of Mum's in the village churchyard but the church had lost the original records of where Mum was buried and the new remembrance area was unsuitable as it was in a different part of the churchyard and Dad himself had commented he did not like it. So it was decided to scatter some of his ashes as near to Mum as memory allowed and take the rest to his birthplace, Malmesbury, and divide them between his parents' grave in the town and that of his brother, Denis, in the outlying village of Charlton.

It should be pointed out that the scattering of ashes without permission is illegal but if we wanted them to be where we wanted and not where the church dictated it had to be a covert operation, and shades of The Great Escape and the disposal of tunnel earth down trouser legs sprung to mind! The first problem was the sheer amount of gleaming white ash!

However, we had split it into manageable amounts and had put the first amount for churchyard usage in a miniature malt whisky tin.

The day was damp and humid, the grass long and very wet as we gathered in the corner of the churchyard and Ken rather furtively emptied the contents in a thin line near to Mum and a few words were said. However, to our horror, when he had finished, the gleaming white line of ash left would have done the centre-line at Wembley proud and surely had become the second man-made object to be seen from the moon, let alone by passing church-wardens! Frantically Ken endeavoured to blend the whiteness into the wet grass with some success, but also with the transfer of much of it to his black shoes! Eventually both shoes and grass returned to normal and we left the scene of our first remembrance, feeling that despite mechanical problems Dad would have approved, albeit with a wry smile.

The hundred mile drive to Wiltshire led us next to the beautiful Cotswold village of Charlton where, after lunch, and in the rain, we went to the ancient churchyard where lies Dad's only brother Denis and his wife Kathleen. Uncle Denis was head gamekeeper to the Earl of Suffolk on his adjacent family estate, Charlton Park, who had died suddenly aged 46, many years ago and whom Dad idolised.

Here the scattering went without a hitch despite the rain; the only witnesses were the ancient trees who had seen it all before as we put the ashes in a convenient hole on the untidy grave under a weary Christmas wreath, not very attractive, but practical. Again we felt Dad's silent approval as we left this idyllic, rural setting.

Thence to Malmesbury, ancient town of King Athelstan, Thomas Hobbes and generations of the Pike family, and the town cemetery again empty but for a gardener strimming in a far corner, where we located the grave of Dad's parents, and our grandparents, Emily and 'Olly,' and the ashes of Dad's elder sister, our Auntie May.

Our intention again had been to dig a small hole in the grave and deposit the remaining ashes in it and to that effect I had brought a small garden hand-fork. However, to our dismay, the grave was covered in dark grey chippings and there were still so many gleaming white ashes! As we had no choice, we scattered them over the chippings leaving them Dulux-shining white and visible for miles!

Trying to blend them in with the fork proved futile and as fickle fate would have it the rain had stopped, so we looked urgently around on surrounding graves, anywhere, for a utensil, vase, urn, whatever, to collect water to wash them in. Spying a pottery jug seemed to have solved the problem so I eagerly filled it and proudly returned for approbation and success only to find it had a hole in it and a reluctant dribble was all it could produce.

Worried now that our rather frenzied activity would attract the gardener's attention, we decided to leave it as it was, but, as if in final approval, fate relented and it started to rain heavily and the last mortal remains of Sydney George Pike, 'Paddy,' 'Bob,' Great-Grandad, Grandad and Dad were slowly but irrevocably and with love returned to the ancient roots he so loved.

For us, we felt Dad would be content: he loved Mum, and in his later years constantly referred to his roots with deep affection; he would have enjoyed overcoming petty bureaucracy and he would have smiled at the black humour of it all – we did what we thought was best because we loved him and will always do so.

ABOUT THE AUTHOR

Robert Edward Pike was born in Charing Cross and lived in South London until his early twenties. He went to Teacher Training College in Leicester and was a Drama teacher for twenty years before ill health forced early retirement. He is married with three children and has lived in Saffron Walden for the last thirty-nine years, where he is known as a local First World War historian. He was the longest serving Editor of 'If You Want the Old Battalion' newsletter of the Essex Western Front Association and has written numerous articles for local newspapers and magazines.He has a mobile home on the Somme, in northern France, and is a member of the Somme branch of the Royal British Legion.

OTHER BOOKS BY
ROBERT EDWARD PIKE

The Victor Heroes

Published by Ancre Books 2000. ISBN 0-9539507-0-0

The story of the 159 men from the Essex market town of Saffron Walden who marched away never to return.

For Still We Hear Them Singing

Published by Grosvenor House 2015. ISBN 978-1-78148-910-9

A book of poems and photos, inspired by the lives and deaths of real people and the need to remember; poems that are often poignant, sometimes humorous, many based on true stories of men from the small market-town of Saffron Walden in rural Essex. They also examine different theatres such as Gallipoli and Palestine and different participants, French, Indian, Italian, Turkish, all who shared a common experience.

The Company of These Fellows

Published by Grosvenor House 2018. ISBN 978-1-78623-338-7

Further poems examining the effect of the Great War on all who lived and died in the 'War for Civilisation.'

Lightning Source UK Ltd.
Milton Keynes UK
UKHW011400260721
387786UK00001B/2